COLLABORATIONS:
ENGLISH IN OUR LIVES

BEGINNING 2 STUDENT BOOK

The publication of *Collaborations* was directed by the members of the Heinle & Heinle Secondary and Adult ESL Publishing Team:

Publisher: Stanley Galek
Editorial Director: Roseanne Mendoza
Production Services Coordinator: Lisa McLaughlin
Market Development Director: Elaine Uzan Leary

Also participating in the publication of the program were:

Director of Production: Elizabeth Holthaus
Assistant Editor: Ann Keefe
Manufacturing Coordinator: Mary Beth Hennebury
Full Service Design and Production: PC&F, Inc.
Illustration Program: Brian Karas and PC&F, Inc.

Manufactured in the United States of America.

ISBN: 0-8384-4107-6

Heinle & Heinle is a division of International Thomson Publishing, Inc.

Photo Credits:

Cover: Jann Huizenga, top, center left; James Higgins, center middle, bottom; Judy Kaul, center right.

Unit 1: FPG, 1; Jann Huizenga, 2, 4, 6, 7, 8, 9, 10, 11, 12, 13 top right, 13 bottom; Ziqiang Shr, 13 top left.

Unit 2: FPG, 17; Sarah Hoskins, 18, 20 left, 21, 22, 24, 25, 31; Peter Stazione, 20 right; Calvin Wharton, 23 top; Michael Johnston, 23 bottom; Jann Huizenga, 26 top right, 26 bottom; Ziqiang Shr, 26 top left; Ken Light, 29.

Unit 3: James Higgins (Higgins & Ross), 35, 36, 42, 44, 45; Jann Huizenga, 39, 47, 49; Judy Kaul, 46 top; Michael Johnston, 46 bottom; Art Murphy, 46 left; Barry Chin, 48.

Unit 4: Silvio Mazzarese, 51; Judy Kaul, 52, 63; Ken Light, 54 left, 55; Nancy Hunter Warren, 54 right; Ann Savino, 58; Jann Huizenga, 59, 60, 65; James Higgins (Higgins & Ross), 64 top; Calvin Wharton, 64 bottom left; Nikos Nafpliotis, 64 bottom right.

Unit 5: The Stock Market/David Brooks, 67; Thieh Nguyen, 68, 72, 73, 74, 75; Betty Lynch, 77; Leah Melnick, 78 top; Jann Huizenga, 78 bottom; Ziqiang Shr, 79.

Unit 6: Phil Hersee, 83; Calvin Wharton, 84, 86, 90 upper middle, 90 lower middle, 95, 97; Janet Melvin, 88 top right, 88 bottom right; Nancy Warner, 88 left; Dolly Huizenga, 89 left; Jann Huizenga, 89 right; Julaine Herraid, 90 bottom.

COLLABORATIONS:
ENGLISH IN OUR LIVES

BEGINNING 2 STUDENT BOOK

Gail Weinstein-Shr
Jann Huizenga

Heinle & Heinle Publishers
A Division of International Thomson Publishing, Inc.
Boston, MA 02116, U.S.A.

The ITP logo is a trademark under license.

CONTENTS

Language Structures	Academic Skills Development	Community Building
• *be* (long and short forms) • *have* • *like / love* + infinitive • *and . . . too* • *should* (for making suggestions)	• finding things in common • comparing • describing • evaluating learning • listening/note-taking	• finding things in common with classmates • bringing in old photos
• present continuous • *do* questions • short answers with *do* and *don't* • adverbs of frequency • preposition of location • *feel* + adjective	• thinking about learning • comparing • analyzing • evaluating learning • brainstorming • listening/note-taking	• learning how classmates like to learn • making collaborative classroom rules
• simple past • past time phrases • *there is/there are* • possessive pronouns • *could* (for making suggestions)	• categorizing • comparing • thinking about cause and result • evaluating learning • listening/note-taking	• sharing ways families have changed • sharing ways to keep native language and culture alive • sharing family photos
• simple present • *be,* present and past • *a/an* • *have to*	• evaluating • classifying • solving problems • brainstorming • evaluating learning • listening/note-taking	• learning about classmates' jobs • sharing information about jobs in the community
• simple present questions and short answers • future with *will* • compound sentences with *or*	• comparing • consulting resources • asking for help • evaluating learning • listening/note-taking	• making a classroom trading post • creating a community resource directory
• *wh* questions (past) • *must / must not* • combining sentences with *and . . . too, and . . . either, and . . . but*	• reacting personally • comparing • brainstorming • advising • evaluating learning • listening/note-taking	• making a class wall display • teaching classmates about one's country • making a group handbook for newcomers

THE WORLD

Do you want to see where the people in this book come from? Their countries are labeled.

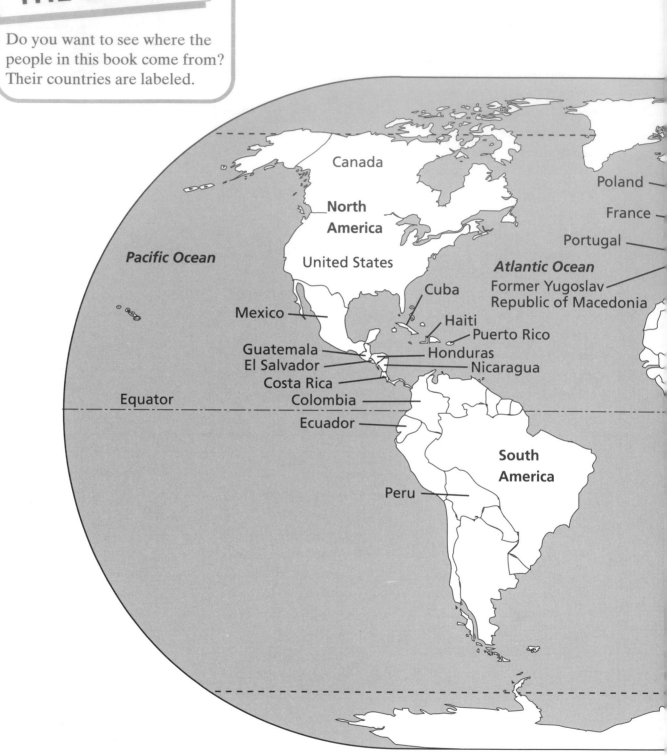

Canada

North America

Pacific Ocean

United States

Poland

France

Portugal

Atlantic Ocean

Cuba

Mexico

Former Yugoslav
Republic of Macedonia

Haiti

Puerto Rico

Guatemala

Honduras

El Salvador

Nicaragua

Costa Rica

Equator

Colombia

Ecuador

South America

Peru

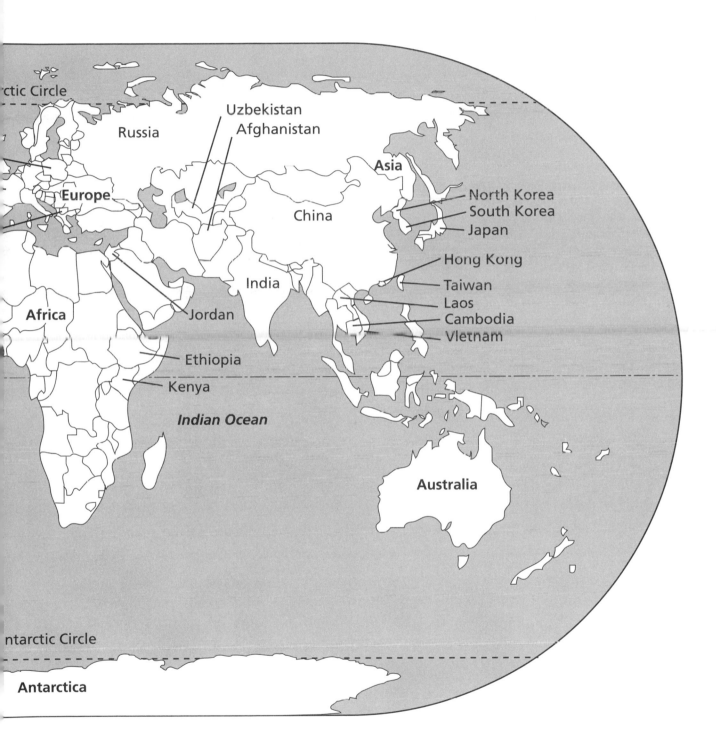

Arctic Circle

Russia

Uzbekistan

Afghanistan

Asia

Europe

China

North Korea

South Korea

Japan

Hong Kong

Taiwan

India

Laos

Africa

Cambodia

Vietnam

Jordan

Ethiopia

Kenya

Indian Ocean

Australia

Antarctic Circle

Antarctica

ABOUT THIS SERIES

Our purpose for creating this series is to provide opportunities for adult immigrants and refugees to develop English language and literacy skills while reflecting, as individuals and with others, on their changing lives.

We believe that the best adult ESL classrooms are places where learners and teachers work collaboratively, talk about issues that matter to them, use compelling materials, and engage in tasks that reflect their life experiences and concerns. We see learning as a process in which students are encouraged to participate actively, and the classroom as a place where students share and reflect on their experiences and rehearse for new roles in the English-speaking world beyond its walls.

How Are the Books in the Series Organized?

Unlike most adult ESL materials, *Collaborations* is not organized around linguistic skills nor life skill competencies, but around contexts for language use in learners' lives. Each student book consists of six units, beginning with the individual and moving out through the series of ever-widening language environments shown below.

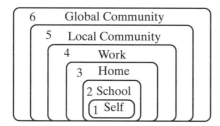

The units revolve around the narratives of newcomers who tell or write of their experiences. Each unit focuses on a particular site in North America, generally one that has a significant number of ESL programs and learners. In some locations, we have chosen a particular ethnic group. In others, we have made the multiethnic character of the area the focal point of the unit. It is our belief that within the marvelous diversity of newcomers, there are seeds for finding sameness—the common threads of experience—as newcomers make sense of managing life in a new setting with new constraints as well as new possibilities.

Grammar, vocabulary development, language functions, and competencies are interwoven throughout the units in each student book. However, the organizing principles are reversed from most traditional materials. Rather than selecting linguistic items and then creating contexts to elicit them, *Collaborations* addresses language development and competencies as they naturally emerge from the contexts and the authentic texts. For those who wish to focus more on specific competencies or language structures, detailed indexes are provided to enable participants to identify where the item is taught, with resources for further practice in the workbook and the teacher's kit.

Collaborations is intended for use with learners of English in adult programs in school districts, community colleges, and community-based programs. While it is an excellent fit in non-credit programs, it may also be the right choice for some credit programs because of its strong emphasis on critical thinking and problem solving. The assessment component for the program—with its placement guidelines and instructions for portfolio assessment as well as more formal quizzes and tests—facilitates adaptation to either program. Particularly at the higher levels of the program, there is an emphasis on development of skills needed in academic programs, GED study, and workplace situations.

What Are the Other Components of *Collaborations*?

The supplementary **workbook** for each level is correlated to the student book. It offers independent study tasks that recycle and reinforce language points from the corresponding units of the student book. Each workbook unit has a predictable structure that contains the following:
- grammar work in context
- extended reading and writing
- vocabulary work
- competency-based tasks
- tests and self assessment

In each unit, the workbook tasks follow the sequence of the activities in the student book and further develop the unit themes.

The **teacher's resource kit** consists of a variety of materials to extend classroom activities and to facilitate and assess learners' progress. The materials listed below are provided in a format that can be inserted into the teacher's kit binder.
- the teacher's edition
- wall maps of the world and of North America
- blackline activity masters
- the assessment program
- overhead transparencies
- cassette tapes

The teacher's edition includes reduced student book pages, suggestions from the authors, insights from field test instructors who used the material in their classes, and space for teachers to keep their own teaching/learning journals. The transparencies are intended to be used for problem-posing activities, Language Experience writing, and oral language practice, among other things.

The assessment program includes traditional benchmarks such as pre-tests, individual unit checks, midterm and final exams, as well as guidelines for developing learner portfolios. The program is meant to encourage learners to set their own goals and monitor their own progress.

Finally, there are two cassette tapes for each level. The classroom tape contains all the stories from each unit of the student book as well as an authentic "review interview," for which there is an accompanying worksheet in the teacher's kit. The student tape contains all of the above with additional listening and repetition activities for use at home or in a lab.

Each unit in the student book is designed to provide at least 10 hours of activities, or 60 hours for the entire book. However, if used in conjunction with the workbook and teacher's kit, each unit provides at least 16 hours of activities for a total of 96 hours.

ABOUT THIS LEVEL

What Is Included in Each Unit?

Each unit in this level includes:

- authentic texts of some kind (photos, student writings, interview material) that have been collected from newcomers throughout the United States and Canada;
- an opportunity to react/respond to those texts and to relate them to personal experience;
- an invitation to master the language of the text by *Playing with Story Language;*
- a task for *Listening In,* in which learners have an opportunity to hear authentic and natural language from their best source of input—their teacher;
- an invitation for *Doing It in English,* in which learners practice functions of English for purposes appropriate to each context;
- a focus on *Ideas for Action,* in which learners reflect critically on their situation and what they can do to act on it;
- an opportunity for *Journal Writing,* which allows learners to react in writing to the themes of the unit and interact on paper with the teacher;
- an interactive *Learning about Each Other* task to foster fluency while building community among learners in the classroom;
- *Other Voices from North America* to provide expanded opportunities for reading and discussion;
- *Options for Learning,* a task in which students choose to study survival skills competencies from a list of competencies (and follow up in worksheets in the teacher's kit);
- an invitation to *Look Back* where learners reflect on what they have learned, what they want to study more about, and which activities suit them the most; and
- a *Checklist for Learning* to provide learners with a way to monitor their own progress, and to review previous material.

USER QUESTIONS ABOUT *COLLABORATIONS*

The language in this book is not as controlled as other materials I've used. Will this be too difficult for my students?

Adults have been learning languages, with and without language instruction, from the time of the first human migration. Students in an English-language setting acquire language most efficiently when there is something worth communicating about. When the building blocks of language are made accessible, acquisition becomes natural and pleasurable. The aim in this series is to provide learners with the tools they need and to create conditions in which communicating is well worth the effort. Because language is a medium for negotiating social relationships, part of the goal is to create a classroom community in which English takes on meaning and purpose. The obstacles learners face because of their incomplete mastery of the English in the material are more than offset by compelling reasons to communicate.

What should I do if my students do not yet know the grammar or vocabulary in the stories and tasks?

Any teacher who has ever faced a class of eager ESL learners has had to grapple with the reality that learners come with differences in their prior exposure to English and with their own individual language-learning timetables, strategies, and abilities. There is no syllabus which will address directly and perfectly the stage of language development of any particular learner, let alone a diverse group. This material reflects the belief that learners can benefit most when forms and functions are made available in the service of authentic communicative tasks. Teaching is most effective when it taps into areas that are ready for development.

For this reason, tasks in *Collaborations* are open-ended and multi-faceted, allowing individuals to make progress according to their current stages of development. The inclusion of numerous collaborative tasks makes it possible for more capable peers as well as instructors to provide assistance to learners as they move to new stages of growth in mastering English.

It is not necessary for learners to understand every word or grammatical structure in order to respond to a story, theme, or issue. The context created by evocative photographs, by familiar situations, and by predictable tasks usually allows learners to make good guesses about meaning even when they do not control all of the vocabulary or structures they see. Any given reading or activity is successful if it evokes a reaction in the learner, and if it creates a situation in which learners are eager to respond. When appropriate language structures and vocabulary are provided toward that end, language acquisition is facilitated. Within this framework, total mastery is not critical: total engagement is.

What do I do about errors my students make?

Errors are a natural part of the language-learning process, as learners test out their hypotheses about how the new language works. Different learners benefit from varying degrees of attention to form and function. For this reason, there are supplementary activities in the workbooks and teacher's kits where learners can give focused attention to vocabulary, grammar, functions, and competencies.

The detailed indexes can also assist users in locating language forms that are of immediate concern to them. Form-focused activities can be used as material for explicit study or practice, as well as for monitoring progress in language development. This series operates on the assumption that the most important ingredient for language acquisition is the opportunity to use English to communicate about things that matter. The supplementary materials will be most effective if the time set aside to focus on form is not seen as an end in and of itself, but rather, is viewed as a necessary component in developing the tools for meaningful communication and classroom community building.

ACKNOWLEDGMENTS

This book would never have been possible without the enthusiastic help of those whose stories grace these pages. We cannot thank them all by name here, but their names appear after each story. We are grateful to colleagues, teachers, and administrators who helped so much in arranging interviews and collecting stories, among them Jean Rose, Susanna Levitt, and Bob Marseille (ABC School, Cerritos, CA); Ana Macias (El Paso Community College, TX); Nancy Gross (LaGuardia Community College, NYC); Marta Pitts (Lindsey Hopkins Technical Education Center, Miami, FL); Leann Howard and Eileen Schmitz (San Diego Community College, CA); Yom Shamash (Invergarry Learning Centre, Vancouver, BC); Adena Staben and Suzanne Liebman (College of Lake County, IL); Jenny Wittner (Chicago Commons, IL); Kit Bell (Metropolitan Skills Center, Los Angeles, CA); Harriet Lindenburg (Santa Fe Community College, NM); and Susan Joyner, Polly Scoville, and Sally Ali (Fairfax County Adult ESL Program, VA).

We thank the many fine photographers whose work is included here. While they are too numerous to name here, we would like to acknowledge those whose work appears repeatedly: Jim Higgins, whose wonderful contributions are central to the book, Ken Light, Nancy Hunter Warren, Mark Neyndorff, Ann Savino, and Sarah Hoskins.

We'd like to thank the members of the original "think tank," Marilyn Gillespie, Jean Handscombe, and Loren McGrail, whose valuable input kicked off the project, as well as our many reviewers along the way. All of whom gave shape to the final product. Our many field testers not only provided important feedback in the final stages but also allowed us to quote them extensively in the Teacher's Edition. We are thankful for their wonderful insights.

At Heinle and Heinle, Jann is grateful to Editorial Director Roseanne Mendoza for her expert guidance not only throughout this project but also in previous projects, *Writing Workout* and *All Talk,* where many of her ideas on ESL materials were developed and seeds for *Collaborations* were sown; to Erik Gunderson, for earlier encouraging the development of her ideas on teaching reading in *Reading Workout;* and to Stan Galek and Charles Heinle for believing in the project through all its ups and downs.

Gail gives special thanks to Chris Foley for the invitation to imagine aloud and to write, and to Erik Gunderson for being an invaluable part of the *Stories* team when many of her own ideas about ESL materials were germinating.

We are both grateful to Ann Keefe, Assistant Editor, for her good nature and help with endless nitty-gritty problems; to Lisa McLaughlin, Production Editor, for her sensational work in producing the series; and to Chris Foley for nurturing the work in its early stages. We'd also like to thank Louise Gelinas and the staff at PC&F for their fine editing and production work.

Last, but not least, the support of our families and friends is warmly appreciated. Jann would like to thank Kim for the laughter and love, John for the education in hard work and fair play, and Dolly for her exuberance and support. Gail is grateful to Z.Q. Shr for world wisdom and endlessly patient help with the computer, to Linda Lee and Jean Bernard-Johnston for their relentless support and lessons in integrity, and to Hannah Rebecca Shr, for sheer joy and perspective on what matters most.

Learning about Each Other in Miami

The stories in this unit come from Miami, Florida. Miami has many newcomers from Cuba, Haiti, and Central and South America.

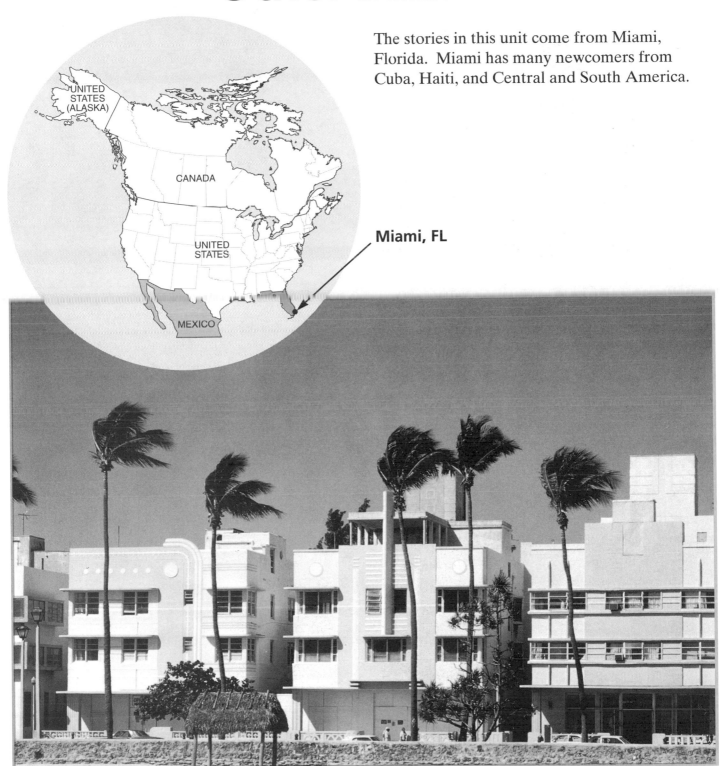

UNITED STATES (ALASKA)

CANADA

UNITED STATES

MEXICO

Miami, FL

A Group Story

All about Us

We all like to laugh.
We all talk a lot.
We all are single.
We all are romantic.
We all have brown eyes.
We all like Miami, but . . .
   we all want to return to our countries.

And we all love to be in photographs!

From left to right: Guy-Charles Emeran is from Haiti. Alexito Leon
   is from Ecuador. Ho Ah-Yi is from Costa Rica. Kattia Aguilar
   is from Costa Rica. They study ESL at Lindsey Hopkins
   Technical Educational Center in Miami.

• What are you and your classmates like?

2 Playing with Story Language

A. Listen to the story.

B. Listen again and write the missing words.

All about Us

We all like to laugh.

We all _____talk_____ a lot.
      1

We all _____ single.
      2

We all _____ romantic.
      3

We all _____ brown eycs.
      4

We all _____ Miami, but . . .
      5

   we all _____ to return to our countries.
      6

And we all _____ to be in photographs!
      7

C. Read the story to a partner. Listen as your partner reads.

D. CHALLENGE: Cover the story. Your teacher or partner will read two sentences from the story. Write them below.

_____

_____

_____

_____

PICTURE DICTIONARY: Words to Describe Us		Add more words with the class.
active	intelligent	
cheerful	rich	
friendly	romantic	
hardworking	sad	
lazy	talkative	

Alexito Leon

I am shy, friendly, talkative, and romantic.
I give my girlfriend a rose each week.

 Which words in the Picture Dictionary describe you?
Tell a partner. Then write.

I am _____, _____,

_____, and _____.

My partner is _____, _____,

_____, and _____.

I am _____, and my partner is too.

4 Listening in: About Our Teacher

A. What is your opinion? Which words describe your teacher? Put a check (✔) next to them.

_____ active	_____ shy
_____ cheerful	_____ rich
_____ friendly	_____ romantic
_____ hardworking	_____ sad
_____ intelligent	_____ talkative
_____ (other)	_____ (other)
_____ (other)	_____ (other)

B. Now listen to your teacher describe herself or himself. Circle the words you hear. Write in others. **Were you right about your teacher?**

 C. Talk to a partner. Compare yourself with your teacher.

Our teacher is talkative, and I am too.

She's romantic, but I'm not.

Be	
Long Form	**Short Form**
I **am**	I**'m**
you **are**	you**'re**
she **is**	she**'s**
he **is**	he**'s**
it **is**	it**'s**
we **are**	we**'re**
they **are**	they**'re**

Doing It in English: Describing What We Look Like

Ho writes:

> We all have brown eyes and black hair. I have wavy hair, and Alexito does too. Kattia has straight hair, and Guy-Charles has curly hair. We are all good-looking!

Guy-Charles   Alexito   Ho   Kattia

Eye Colors	Hair Colors	Hair Descriptions
brown	brown	long
blue	black	short
green	red	curly
gray	blond	wavy
	gray	straight

Have	
I **have** you **have** we **have** they **have**	he **has** she **has** it **has**

Describe the eyes and hair of three classmates.
Don't write their names.

Example: _____ He has blue eyes and curly, brown hair. _____

1. _____

2. _____

3. _____

Now read your sentences to the class. Can your classmates guess who you are describing?

6 Journal Writing

A dialogue journal is a small notebook where you can have a conversation in writing with your teacher.

In your journal, write to your teacher about yourself. Answer these questions: **Where do you live? Where are you from? What are you like?** Ask your teacher a question, too.

This is what Monica Cabrera wrote. She studies ESL in Miami with the students on page 6.

I am Monica Cabrera. I live in Miami, Florida. I'm from Lima, Peru. I have a big family there.

I'm shy. But I am also impulsive. I get angry easily. Do you ever get angry?

M.

This is how her teacher answered.

I am Monica Cabrera. I live in Miami, Florida. I'm from Lima, Peru. I have a big family there.

I'm shy. But I am also impulsive. I get angry easily. Do you ever get angry?

M.

Yes, I get angry when people break their promises! I have a big family too. How many do you have in your family?

K.

IDIOM
break a promise

7 More Stories from Miami

Read more about Kattia and Guy-Charles, students from the Miami class.
Try to find something that **you** have in common with each one.
Underline it.

I'm Kattia Aguilar. I'm from Costa Rica. I'm 21 years old and single.

I love to dance salsa. Sometimes Alexito and I dance during break!

I like to cook, too, but I don't like to clean the kitchen.

I try to be strong, but I'm sensitive and sentimental.

Kattia Aguilar (left) studies ESL at Lindsey Hopkins Technical Educational Center in Miami.

My name is Guy-Charles Emeran and I'm from Haiti.

I'm friendly and well-educated. With women, I'm a real gentleman. My parents taught me well.

I like to sit and talk to people. When people get to know me well, they see I'm very different from others.

Guy-Charles Emeran studies ESL at Lindsey Hopkins Technical Educational Center in Miami.

What do you like to do? What do you love to do?

 Circle new words in the stories. Talk to a partner about the words. Read one story aloud to a partner.

Like and Love
I like **to cook.**
I like **to play chess.**
I love **to read.**
I love **to walk.**

Learning about Each Other: Finding Things in Common

 Work with a small group. Like the Miami group, find things that you all have in common. Elect a group secretary and write as many sentences as you can.

All about Us

Read your story to other groups or put all the stories on the walls of your classroom.

All about Us

We all like to laugh.
We all talk a lot.
We all are single.
We all are romantic.
We all have brown eyes.
We all like Miami, but . . .
    we all want to return to our countries.

And we all love to be in photographs!

9 Then and Now: Talking about Changes

Have you changed since you came to North America?
Write three sentences. Follow the examples below, if you wish.

Before, I *had* long hair.   Now, I *have* short hair.
Before, I *was* talkative.   Now, I *am* shy.

1. _____

   _____

2. _____

   _____

3. _____

   _____

 Read your sentences to a partner. Listen to your partner's sentences and
ask questions.

10 Bringing the Outside in: Old Photos

Bring to class an old photograph of yourself, perhaps
one from your native country. In a small group, show
your photos. Describe how you are similar to or
different from the *old* you.

Roberto and I are in a hurry to learn English. We speak Spanish outside of class. Almost everyone in Miami speaks Spanish, so it's hard to practice English.

Miguel Hernandez (right) is from Colombia. Roberto Mejia is from Honduras. They study ESL at Lindsey Hopkins Technical Educational Center in Miami.

IDIOM
be in a hurry

What should Miguel and Roberto do?
With the class, write some suggestions.

1.   They should join a club or group where people speak English.

2. _____

3. _____

4. _____

Should
I You She He We They } **should join** a club.
Use **should** to make suggestions.

12 Other Voices from North America

Choose one or two stories to read. Is the writer like you or someone you know? Tell a partner.

My name is Dirk Xu. I am from China. I live in Amherst, Massachusetts. I'm 58 years old.

I like to smoke a pipe, as you can see. I also like to make watercolor paintings.

Dirk Xu studies English at Greenfield Community College in Massachusetts.

I am Dominika Szmerdt. I'm single. I'm not a rich person. Material things are not important to me. I love to read books, and I spend all my money on them.

In Poland, when I was younger, I did not think about money. But now, I am preoccupied with saving money for rent, food, and clothes. But I still believe that the best things in life are free.

Dominika Szmerdt studies at the University of Colorado in Boulder, CO.

My name is Stela Jovicic. I am divorced with one child. I am very strong, and I can face any hardship.

Before my baby, I liked to read books, play sports, and enjoy all the nature around me.

But now I am too busy taking care of my child and working.

Stela Jovicic is from the former Yugoslav Republic of Macedonia. She studies English in New York City.

WORDS I WANT TO REMEMBER

13 Options for Learning: English with New People

A. How do you want to use English around new friends and strangers?
Check (✔) your answers.

	Already Do	Want to Learn	Not Interested
To introduce myself	————	————	————
To make small talk with strangers	————	————	————
To slow down speakers	————	————	————
To invite a new friend to do something	————	————	————
(Other) —————	————	————	————
—————	————	————	————

B. Talk to a partner or group about your learning goals. Use your native language if you wish. Tell the class in English.

C. Ask your teacher for a *Collaborations* worksheet on one of these goals.

14 Looking Back

Think about your learning. Fill in the blanks. Then tell the class your ideas.

A. In this unit I learned _____

_____ .

B. I want to study more about _____ .

C. The activity I liked best was 1 2 3 4 5 6 7 8 9 10 11 12 13

because _____ .

D. The activity I liked least was 1 2 3 4 5 6 7 8 9 10 11 12 13

because _____ .

Checklist for Learning

I. **Vocabulary:** Check (✔) the words you know. Add more words if you wish.

Words to Describe People

_____ shy
_____ rich
_____ romantic
_____ lazy
_____ hardworking
_____ active
_____ friendly
_____ intelligent
_____ talkative
_____ cheerful
_____ sad
_____ strong
_____ sensitive
_____ sentimental
_____ impulsive
_____ well-educated

_____ _____
_____ _____
_____ _____

Words to Describe Hair

_____ long
_____ short
_____ wavy
_____ curly
_____ straight

_____ _____

Colors

_____ brown
_____ blue
_____ green
_____ gray
_____ black
_____ red

_____ _____

IDIOMS

_____ break a promise
_____ be in a hurry

II. **Language:** Check (✔) what you can do in English. Add more ideas if you wish.

I can

_____ describe someone's hair and eyes.
_____ describe my personality.
_____ write about myself.
_____ compare myself with others using **but.**
_____ read short stories.

_____ _____
_____ _____

III. **Listening:** Listen to the Review Interview at the end of Unit 1. Ask your teacher for the *Collaborations* worksheet.

Unit 2

Ways of Learning and Teaching: Stories from Chicago

The stories in this unit come from the Chicago area. Chicago, Illinois, attracts newcomers from all over the world, especially Mexico, Poland, India, the Philippines, and Russia.

Chicago, IL

Eliseo del Rio's Story

In Adena's class, we always talk about interesting topics. Sometimes we play language games. I never feel bored. The time always goes very fast. In this photo, Adena is teaching us new vocabulary words.

This class is not only about English. It's about us!

Eliseo del Rio is from Mexico. He studies with teacher Adena Staben at the College of Lake County, near Chicago. He is sitting on the far right in the photograph. He has a mustache.

• How do you learn best?

2 Playing with Story Language

A. Listen to the story.

B. Listen again and write the words in the correct order.

1. In this class _____ *we talk about* _____ many topics.

   we   about   talk

2. Sometimes _____ games.

   play   language   we

3. I _____ bored.

   feel   never

4. The time _____ fast.

   very   goes   always

5. In this photo, Adena _____ vocabulary words.

   us   teaching   new   is

C. Read the story to a partner. Listen as your partner reads.

D. **CHALLENGE:** Cover the story. Your teacher or partner will read two sentences from the story. Write them below.

_____

_____

_____

_____

_____

_____

Doing It in English: Talking about Classrooms

A. The photos on these pages show English classrooms in the Chicago area. **What are the students doing? What is the teacher doing?** Talk with the class. The Picture Dictionary may help.

Present Continuous	
I *am* read*ing*	He *is* read*ing*
You *are* read*ing*	She *is* read*ing*
We *are* read*ing*	They *are* read*ing*

PICTURE DICTIONARY: Ways of Working

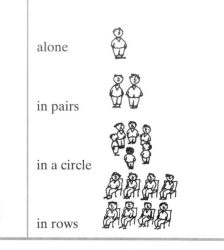

listening

speaking

reading

writing

sitting

standing

in a small group

in a large group

alone

in pairs

in a circle

in rows

1

2

4

3

B. Look again at the photos. How do you think the students feel?
Write your answers. The Picture Dictionary below may help.

PICTURE DICTIONARY: Opposite Feelings	**Add more words with the class.**

happy   unhappy
 	
      tired   awake
 	
bored   interested
 	
      nervous relaxed	

In photo 1, the students feel _____.

In photo 2, the student feels _____.

In photo 3, the students feel _____.

In photo 4, the students feel _____.

In our class, the students feel _____.

 Talk to a partner. Compare your answers. Tell why you wrote each word.

Listening in: Classroom Arrangements

A. Listen as your teacher talks about Adena's classroom.

Where is the blackboard?
Where is the map?
Where are the students sitting?
Where is Eliseo sitting?
Where is Adena standing?

Prepositions
next to
behind
in front of
around
on

B. How is Adena's classroom similar to your classroom? How is it
different? Write sentences with the class.

Examples: In both classrooms, there is a blackboard in front of the room.
In Adena's class, students sit around tables. We sit behind desks.

Which classroom do you like better? Do you want to move things in
your classroom? Talk with the class.

5 Then and Now: Comparing Classes

Read about what happens in Adena Staben's classroom in Chicago. Are her classes like classes in your country? In the right-hand column, write **SAME** or **DIFFERENT.**

In Adena's Class	In Your Country
Students ask many questions.	
Students work together in groups.	
Students tell the teacher what they want to learn.	
Students ask the teacher for help.	
Students talk a lot.	
Students use the teacher's first name.	
The teacher wants students to talk.	
The teacher is very friendly.	
The teacher likes to learn things from students.	
The teacher uses students' first names.	

Compare your answers with a partner's. Talk about classes in your country. How are they different from classes here? How are they the same?

Tell the class.

In my country, students don't talk much. They listen.

In my country, the teachers are friendly, too.

6 Journal Writing

Teach your teacher! Write something about school in your country. Ask your teacher what he or she thinks.

In China, the teachers are very strict. Students never eat in class! Do you think it's OK when students eat in your class?

Min Hua—I don't really like students to eat in my class. Did you feel surprised when you saw students eat?

GWS

More Stories from the Chicago Area

Read the two stories about teachers. What do **you** think is important in a teacher? Talk about the stories with the class.

The first time I met my teacher Adena, she acted so friendly. She smiled all the time. Everyone in our class is relaxed because she's so friendly. Adena teaches us adult words. Before, I only knew easy words like a child.

Adena must have a good memory. She remembers everybody's name. I was a teacher in Taiwan, and I know how difficult that is. But it makes everybody feel good.

Ruth Chang is from Taiwan. She studies with Adena Staben at the College of Lake County near Chicago. She is on the far left in the photo. Adena is on the far right.

We have a small class. I like it because I get lots of personal attention from our teacher.

Our teacher respects us. She dresses nicely. I think it is important how teachers dress. If they dress formally, students will be respectful of them. If they wear old jeans, small blouses, and punk hair styles, students will not take them seriously. Once I had a teacher like that. He wore jeans with holes in the knees. I thought it was not appropriate.

Jose Tamoyo is from Mexico. He studies at the Chicago Commons. He is sitting in the middle of his class in the photo.

IDIOM
take someone
(or something)
seriously

Circle new words in the stories. Talk to a partner about the words. Read one story aloud to a partner.

8 Other Voices from North America

Choose one or two stories to read. Is the writer like you or someone you know? Tell a partner.

One thing that helps me to learn English is to study in a quiet place. Also, I talk to American people, read a lot of books, listen to tapes, and watch T.V.

I try not to think too much and to enjoy my life. I learn much better if I relax and have fun.

Phala Leng is from Cambodia. She studies at Greenfield Community College in Massachusetts.

In my classroom, I have three rules.

1. Ask questions
2. Ask questions
3. Don't quit!

Hal Stevens is an ESL teacher at Rancho Santiago Community College in Santa Ana, CA.

IDIOM
feel close to someone

WORDS I WANT TO REMEMBER

I had an English teacher in Japan. Her name was Ms. Almond. One day, she had class at Kentucky Fried Chicken. All the students were surprised. But we could talk about many things while eating. We felt close to her.

Ms. Almond always asked "why, why?" in every class. "Why do you have that answer? Why do you think that?" She always wanted students to discuss things. Japanese teachers usually just lecture. At first I was embarrassed for her. But then I started to enjoy her class.

Makiko Imai studies ESL in Los Alamos, NM.

9 Learning about Each Other: Ways We Like to Learn

A. Answer these questions. Then ask a partner the questions.

	Me		My Partner	
	YES	**NO**	**YES**	**NO**
1. Do you like to learn alone?	❏	❏	❏	❏
2. Do you like to learn with a group?	❏	❏	❏	❏
3. Do you like to go fast?	❏	❏	❏	❏
4. Do you like to go slowly?	❏	❏	❏	❏
5. Do you like to learn with a group?	❏	❏	❏	❏
6. Do you like to learn by speaking?	❏	❏	❏	❏
7. Do you like to learn by reading?	❏	❏	❏	❏
8. Do you like to learn by writing?	❏	❏	❏	❏

B. Walk around the classroom. Ask questions. Find two people who say, "Yes, I do" to each question. Write their names.

> Do you like to learn alone?
>
> Yes, I do.
>
> Do you like to learn with a group?
>
> No, I don't.

	Classmate One	**Classmate Two**
1. Do you like to learn alone?		
2. Do you like to learn with a group?		
3. Do you like to go fast?		
4. Do you like to go slowly?		
5. Do you like to learn by listening?		
6. Do you like to learn by speaking?		
7. Do you like to learn by reading?		
8. Do you like to learn by writing?		

A. In your class, how do you talk? How does your teacher talk?

Work in a small group. Together, choose a word from the box for each sentence. Write it in the blank.

Adverbs of Frequency		
always		100%
often		
sometimes		
rarely		
never		0%

1. Our teacher _____ talks.

2. Our teacher _____ asks questions.

3. Our teacher _____ speaks English.

4. Our teacher _____ speaks our language.

5. The students in our class _____ talk.

6. The students in our class _____ ask questions.

7. The students in our class _____ speak English.

8. The students in our class _____ speak our own languages.

B. Talk with the class. Are you happy with the way your class uses language? Tell the class what you like and what you want to change in the class. Ask your teacher's opinion.

11 Options for Learning: English at School

In class, I always use my dictionary. I am afraid to ask questions when I don't understand. But when I read my dictionary, I don't hear what my teacher is saying.

I want to use more English. I want to use less Spanish in class.

Alejandro Gomez is from Mexico.
He lives in San Francisco, CA.

© Ken Light

A. How do you want to use English in the classroom? Check (✔) your answers. Add other ideas if you wish.

	Already Do	Want to Learn	Not Interested
To greet my classmates	_____	_____	_____
To ask permission in class	_____	_____	_____
To read signs at school	_____	_____	_____
To use an index	_____	_____	_____
(Other) _____	_____	_____	_____
_____	_____	_____	_____

B. Talk to a partner or group about your learning goals. Use your native language if you wish. Tell the class in English.

C. Ask your teacher for a *Collaborations* worksheet on one of these goals.

Collaborations: Making Classroom Rules

A. An ESL class at the Chicago Commons made these rules for their classroom. Teacher Lisa Berman wrote them on the blackboard. Do you agree or disagree with these rules?

Check (✔) the boxes.

	I Agree	I Disagree
1.	☐	☐
2.	☐	☐
3.	☐	☐
4.	☐	☐
5.	☐	☐
6.	☐	☐
7.	☐	☐
8.	☐	☐

1. Students should talk a lot in class.
2. Students should listen to each other.
3. Students shouldn't be afraid to make mistakes.
4. Students shouldn't correct each other.
5. Teachers should speak slowly.
6. Teachers should use our language sometimes.
7. Teachers shouldn't be angry when we don't understand.
8. Teacher's shouldn't give too much homework.

Should and Shouldn't

I You She He We They	**should ask** for help in class. **shouldn't be** afraid in class.

Use **should** and **shouldn't** to make rules and suggestions.

B. Work with a small group. Make rules for your class. You may copy Lisa's class rules, or make new rules. Tell the class.

1. The students should

_____

_____

2. The students shouldn't

_____

_____

3. The teacher should

_____

_____

4. The teacher shouldn't

_____

13 Ideas for Action: Learning In and Out of Class

A. How can you learn English in or out of class? Jenny Wittner's class at the Chicago Commons had these suggestions.

Check (✔) the ones you have tried.

_____ **1.** Speak only English at school.

_____ **2.** Read ads and newspapers, watch T.V.

_____ **3.** Listen to music and read the words.

_____ **4.** Try using new words.

_____ **5.** Watch the news in Spanish, then in English.

_____ **6.** Ask questions in class.

_____ **7.** Copy what you read.

_____ **8.** Talk to people in stores.

B. With the class, think of other ways to practice English.

By talking   to whom?   _____

                                      _____

By listening   to what?   _____

                                      _____

By reading   what?   _____

                                      _____

By writing   what?   _____

                                      _____

C. What strategy will you use today? Check (✔) one and tell the class.

14 Bringing the Outside in: Interview Results

Interview a friend who learned English. Ask about the ways he or she practiced. Write the answers here. Tell the class what you learned.

My friend talked to
My friend listened to
My friend read
My friend wrote

15 Looking Back

Think about your learning. Fill in the blanks. Then tell the class your ideas.

A. In this unit I learned _____

_____.

B. I want to study more about _____.

C. The activity I liked best was 1 2 3 4 5 6 7 8 9 10 11 12 13 14

because _____.

D. The activity I liked least was 1 2 3 4 5 6 7 8 9 10 11 12 13 14

because _____.

Checklist for Learning

I. Vocabulary: Check (✔) the words you know. Add more words if you wish.

Frequency Words

_____ always
_____ often
_____ sometimes
_____ rarely
_____ never

_____ _____

Location Words

_____ on
_____ around
_____ next to
_____ behind
_____ in front of

_____ _____

_____ _____

Feeling Words

_____ tired
_____ bored
_____ nervous
_____ afraid
_____ relaxed
_____ happy
_____ unhappy
_____ awake
_____ interested

_____ _____

_____ _____

IDIOMS

_____ take someone (or something) seriously
_____ feel close to someone

II. Language: Check (✔) what you can do in English. Add more ideas if you wish.

I can

_____ express my feelings.
_____ describe my classroom.
_____ think about how I learn best.
_____ talk about learning English.
_____ write classroom rules.
_____ read short stories.

_____ _____

_____ _____

III. Listening: Listen to the Review Interview at the end of Unit 2. Ask your teacher for a *Collaborations* worksheet.

Unit 3

Changing Families, Changing Lives: Stories from Massachusetts

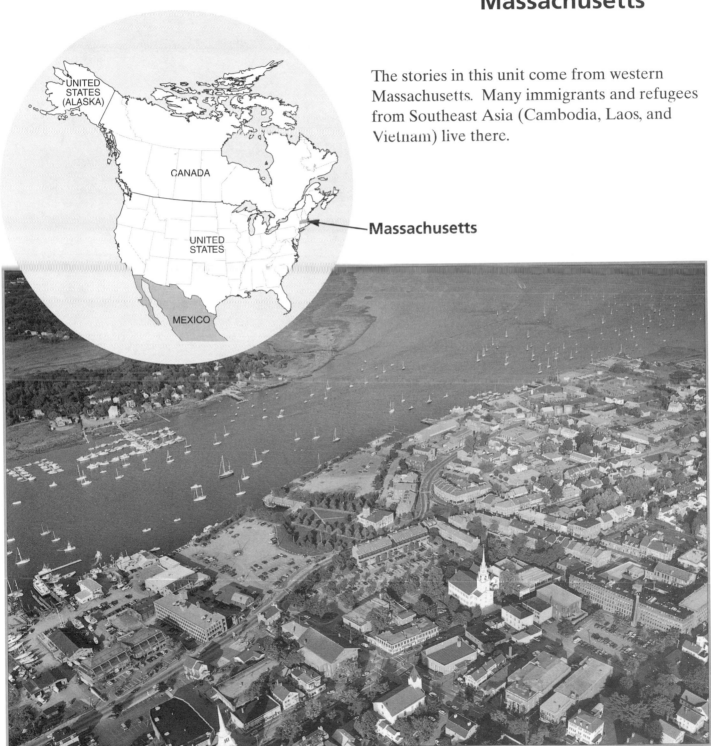

The stories in this unit come from western Massachusetts. Many immigrants and refugees from Southeast Asia (Cambodia, Laos, and Vietnam) live there.

UNITED STATES (ALASKA)

CANADA

UNITED STATES

Massachusetts

MEXICO

Mrs. Khaxoyo's Story

When we got to America, my sons began to grow faster. Sports and American food made them grow tall. Before, in Laos, they liked our Lao food, and they ate everything. Now they don't like our Lao food anymore. They like McDonald's, and they drink lots of Pepsi.

Mrs. Khaxoyo is in back on the left in the photo. The Khaxoyo family is from Laos and lives in Massachusetts.

- Are you changing?
- Is your family changing?

2 Playing with Story Language

A. Listen to the story.

B. Listen to each line again, and repeat.

C. Cover the story on page 36. Listen and write the missing words.

When we ____got____ to America, my sons _____ to grow faster.
                1   2

Sports and American food _____ them grow tall. Before, in Laos, they
                              3

_____ our Lao food, and they _____ everything. Now, they
      4   5

don't _____ our Lao food anymore. They _____
          6   7

McDonald's, and they _____ lots of Pepsi.
                          8

D. Work with a partner. One person reads the story above. The other person covers the story and writes the missing words below. Reverse roles.

When we _____ to America, my sons _____ to grow faster.
              1   2

Sports and American food _____ them grow tall. Before, in Laos, they
                              3

_____ our Lao food, and they _____ everything. Now, they
      4   5

don't _____ our Lao food anymore. They _____
          6   7

McDonald's, and they _____ lots of Pepsi.
                          8

E. Check your answers.

3 Doing It in English: Talking about Food

Mrs. Khaxoyo's sons **like** hamburgers, but they **don't like** Lao food.

What foods do you like and not like? Make two lists. The dictionary below can help.

I like

I don't like

PICTURE DICTIONARY: Foods	**Add more words with the class.**
chicken pizza coffee rice fish salad hamburgers sandwiches ice cream soup	

Tell the class what you like and don't like. In your class, which foods are the most popular? Which foods are the least popular?

I like fish, but I don't like hamburgers.

4 Doing It in English: Talking about Health

Mrs. Khaxoyo's sons eat hamburgers and drink Pepsi. Mrs. Khaxoyo said, **"American food made them grow tall."**

What do you think? Are hamburgers and Pepsi good for you? Do you agree with Mrs. Khaxoyo?

Make lists of healthy and unhealthy foods and drinks. Use words from this box or any other words you know.

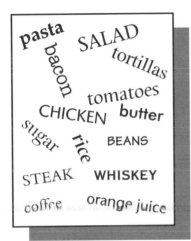

Healthy Foods and Drinks	Unhealthy Foods and Drinks
_____	_____
_____	_____
_____	_____

Do you eat healthy foods? Tell a partner.

5 Bringing the Outside in: Food Containers

Show the class what your family eats. Bring in a bag, a box, or a can from a supermarket or restaurant. In groups, look at the food words. Make lists below.

Words I Know	New Words

Which of the items are good for you? Which are not good for you? Which are expensive? Which are cheap? Make a chart with your class.

6 Then and Now: Comparing Eating Habits

A. Compare what you ate in your country and what you eat now.

Food I Ate in My Country	Do You Eat It Here?
1. _____	often sometimes rarely never
2. _____	often sometimes rarely never
3. _____	often sometimes rarely never
4. _____	often sometimes rarely never

 Tell your answers to a partner or the class. Tell why.

In Mexico, I often ate mangoes, but here I never eat them. They are expensive!

B. How are your eating habits changing?
Complete these sentences.

Before, in my country, I ate _____,

 but now, in this country, I eat _____.

Before, I drank _____,

 but now, I drink _____.

Before, my family cooked _____,

 but now, we cook _____.

 Which country's food do you like best? Is this the same for other people in your family? Tell a partner.

I like Russian food best, but my son prefers American food.

I like our Ethiopian food best!

C. How else are you changing? Fill in the chart.

Now	Before
I live with _____.	I lived with _____.
I live near _____.	I lived near _____.
I like to _____.	I liked to _____.
I buy _____.	I bought _____.
I wear _____.	I wore _____.
I _____ (other).	I _____.

D. Listen as your partner tells you what he or she wrote in Exercise C. Write your partner's answers below. Ask questions as you listen and write.

Could you repeat that please?

Time Phrases with Simple Past

Before, I lived with my family.
Two years ago, I lived with my family.
In 1993, I lived with my family.

Simple Past
Regular Verbs
cook — cooked
like — liked
live — lived
want — wanted
Irregular Verbs
buy — bought
begin — began
drink — drank
eat — ate
go — went
get — got
grow — grew
wear — wore

About My Partner

Now	Before
She/he lives with _____.	She/he lived with _____.
She/he lives near _____.	She/he lived near _____.
She/he likes to _____.	She/he liked to _____.
She/he buys _____.	She/he bought _____.
She/he wears _____.	She/he wore _____.
She/he _____ (other).	She/he _____.

This is my
husband, Ly.

This is me.
I'm Ann Khaxoyo.

This is our
daughter Sumaly.

These are our sons,
Alex (left),
Kenny (center)
and Vi (right).

My mother and father are in Laos.

Possessive Pronouns
(I) — my
(you) — your
(he) — his
(she) — her
(we) — our
(they) — their

Make a chart of Mrs. Khaxoyo's family. Guess how old they are.

Name	Relation to Mrs. Khaxoyo	Age
Alex	son	16 or 17

 With a partner, talk about each person's age.

What do you
think? How old is
Alex?

Maybe he is
16 or 17 years
old.

Listening in: Your Teacher's Family

Look at a photo or drawing of your teacher's family. Listen as your teacher tells about each person. Fill in the chart. Ask questions if you don't understand.

Excuse me. Did you say 23?

Name	Relation to Your Teacher	Age	Other Information

What do you want to know about your teacher's family?
Ask a question.

Where do your parents live?

Learning about Each Other: Our Families

Take out your family photo(s) OR draw your family here.

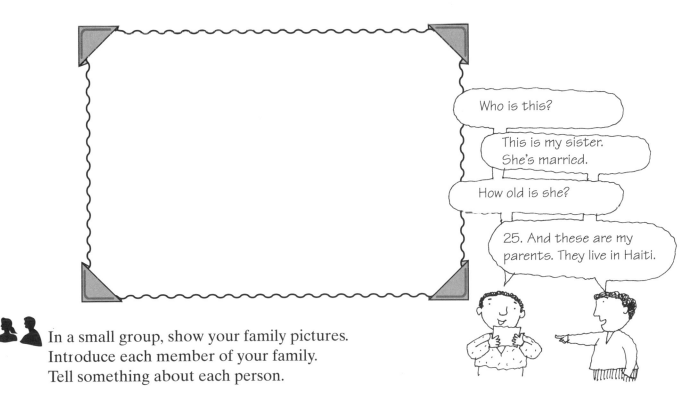

Who is this?

This is my sister. She's married.

How old is she?

25. And these are my parents. They live in Haiti.

In a small group, show your family pictures.
Introduce each member of your family.
Tell something about each person.

More Stories from Massachusetts

Read the two stories about changing. Are any of the people like you or like someone you know? Tell the class.

My grandmother says, "If my country is free, I want to go back." But my sister and I like it here. Even if my country is free, I won't go back. I will stay here. This is my home now.

Su Yin (left) and her family live in Lowell, MA. They are from Cambodia.

IDIOM
go back

  Who in your family wants to stay? Who wants to go back? Tell a partner.

We know Lao music, but we like American music better. We like the beat of American music. We like heavy metal groups like Kiss. Right now our group just plays for fun, but you never know. . . . Maybe we will be rock stars!

The name of this band is "The Pink and the Purple." The four band members are from Laos, and they live in Lowell, MA.

What music do you like best? Bring a tape to share with your class.

 Circle new words in the stories. Talk to a partner about the words.
Read one story aloud to a partner.

Choose one or two stories to read.
Is the writer like you or someone
you know? Tell a partner.

WORDS I WANT TO REMEMBER

When my kids started speaking English to me, I was
mad at them. They said, "I don't know how to speak
Spanish." I said, "You are Mexican. How can you forget
Spanish? It's not right. You have to learn both
languages." But my son didn't.

Gloria Sierra studies English in Bernalillo, NM.

IDIOM
be mad at
(someone)

I come from a Mennonite family. The
Mennonites believe in very simple living.
My ancestors moved from Germany to
the Valley near Philadelphia almost 300
years ago. My parents, brother, and
sisters still live there.

But I have moved to the other side of
the U.S., thousands of miles away. I still
believe in simple living. But I have
changed a lot. My family believes that
women should cover their heads and obey
men. I do not. It would be difficult now
for me to go back to their way of living.

Erma Stauffer lives in San Francisco, CA.

When my great-grandmother arrived
from Poland, she couldn't speak English. My
mother and my aunt didn't learn Yiddish.
All three lived in the same house together,
but they couldn't talk to each other. My
aunt cried when she told me this story.

Gail Weinstein-Shr lives in San Francisco, CA.
She is an author of this book.

12 Thinking about Language Use: At Home

In your home, who speaks English? Who speaks your language?
Make a chart. Tell about the people in your family.

Name	Age	Relation to You	Favorite Language

Show your chart to a partner. Then discuss these questions:
Which language is used most in your home?
Since you began learning English, has anything changed in your family?

13 Options for Learning: English at Home

We like to use Spanish at home.
But sometimes my daughter asks for help with her
homework, and I can't help her. That's why
I'm studying English.

Natividad Pinon studies ESL at
Santa Fe Community College
In New Mexico. He
is from Mexico.

A. How do you want to use English in your home? Check (✔)
your answers. Add other ideas if you wish.

	Already Do	Want to Learn	Not Interested
To write a note to my child's teacher	_____	_____	_____
To write a complaint note to the landlord	_____	_____	_____
To receive phone calls and take messages	_____	_____	_____
To read medicine bottle labels	_____	_____	_____
Other _____	_____	_____	_____

B. Talk to your classmate or your group about your learning goals. You may
use your language if you wish. Tell the class in English.

C. Ask your teacher for a *Collaborations* worksheet on one of these goals.

Vera Tong Tith teaches Khmer (the Cambodian language) to children in Lowell, MA. She says, "Cambodian parents don't want their kids to forget Khmer. So they send the children to this school."

Children learn English fast. Sometimes they forget their native culture and language. What could parents do to help children remember?

Write ideas with your class.

1. _Parents could send their kids to a bilingual school._

2. _____

3. _____

4. _____

Can and Could
Parents **can** send their kids to a bilingual school. Parents **could** send their kids to a bilingual school.
Use **can** and **could** to make suggestions.

15 Journal Writing

Are you changing? If your family is here, are they changing? How?

Write to your teacher about yourself and your family.
Ask your teacher about his or her family.

This is what Maria Medina
from Los Angeles wrote.

My family is changing.
My brother and I like
American food. We
listen to American
music—not Mexican
music. But we always
speak Spanish at
home.

16 Looking Back

Think about your learning. Fill in the blanks. Then tell the class your ideas.

A. In this unit I learned _____

_____.

B. I want to study more about _____.

C. The activity I liked best was 1 2 3 4 5 6 7 8 9 10 11 12 13 14 15

because _____.

D. The activity I liked least was 1 2 3 4 5 6 7 8 9 10 11 12 13 14 15

because _____.

Checklist for Learning

I. Vocabulary: Check (✔) the words you know. Add more words if you wish.

Food Words

_____ soda
_____ coffee
_____ whiskey
_____ pasta
_____ rice
_____ French fries
_____ hamburger
_____ potato chips

_____ _____
_____ _____

Verbs

_____ buy—bought
_____ begin—began
_____ cook—cooked
_____ drink—drank
_____ eat—ate
_____ go—went
_____ get—got
_____ grow—grew
_____ like—liked
_____ live—lived
_____ want—wanted
_____ wear—wore

Family Words

_____ father
_____ mother
_____ wife
_____ husband
_____ sister
_____ brother
_____ son
_____ daughter
_____ grandmother
_____ grandfather

_____ _____
_____ _____

Possessive Pronouns

_____ my
_____ her
_____ his
_____ our
_____ your
_____ their

IDIOMS

_____ go back
_____ be mad at someone

II. Language: Check (✔) what you can do in English. Add more ideas if you wish.

I can

_____ list some healthy and unhealthy foods.
_____ introduce my family.
_____ talk about changes in my life.
_____ tell what foods I like and don't like.
_____ read short stories.
_____ read some words on a food package.
_____ tell some things about my family.

III. Listening: Listen to the Review Interview at the end of Unit 3. Ask your teacher for the *Collaborations* worksheet.

Unit 4

Work That Suits You: Stories from the Southwest

The stories in this unit come from the Southwest. Many Mexicans and Mexican Americans live in the southwestern states of Texas, New Mexico, and Arizona.

Southwestern United States

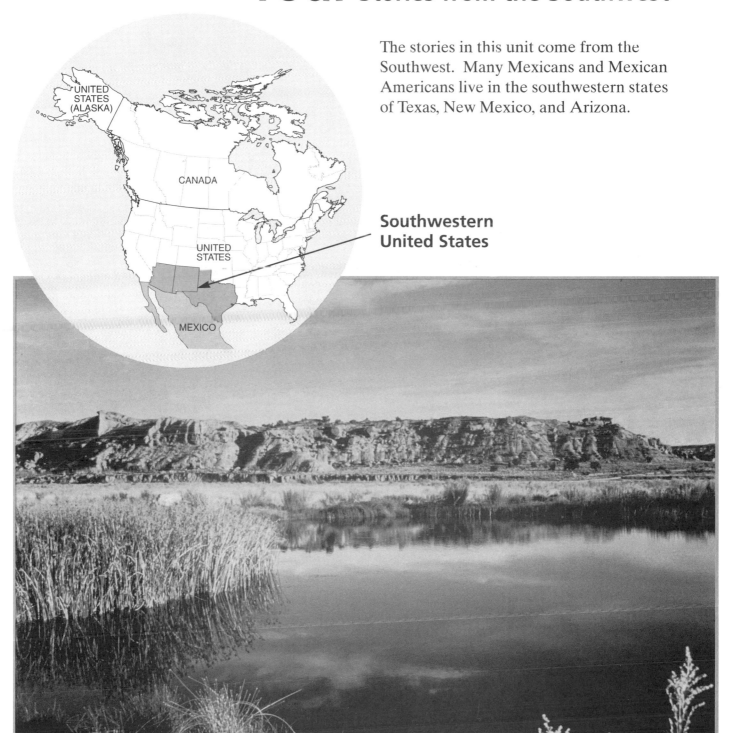

Gloria Sierra's Story

I'm a school bus driver. I like it. I earn $10.00 an hour. I work every morning from 7:00 to 9:00 and in the afternoon from 3:00 to 5:00. I drive American Indian kids. I have a lot of responsibility. I have never had an accident. (Knock on wood!)

Sometimes the kids run around on the bus. Sometimes they stick their hands out the windows. They think I'm too old to notice. I have to watch my two mirrors all the time. I need an eye in the back of my head.

Gloria Sierra lives in Bernalillo, NM. She came to the U.S. from Mexico 30 years ago.

IDIOM
knock on wood

• Would you like this job? Why or why not?

• Do you like your work?* Why or why not?

• What is hard about *your* work?

_____
*on the job, at school, or at home

2 Playing with Story Language

A. Listen to the story.

B. Listen again and write in the missing words.

I'm a school bus driver. I ___like___ it. I _____ $10.00 an
                                   1   2

hour. I _____ every morning from 7:00 to 9:00 and in the afternoon
               3

from 3:00 to 5:00. I _____ American Indian kids. I _____ a
                      4   5

lot of responsibility. I have never had an accident.

    Sometimes the kids _____ around on the bus. Sometimes they
                                  6

_____ their hands out the windows. They _____ I'm too
        7   8

old to notice. I have to watch my two mirrors all the time. I _____ an
                                                              9

eye in the back of my head.

Show your answers to a partner. Do you agree? Check your own answers.

C. Read the story to a partner. Listen as your partner reads.

D. **Challenge:** Your teacher or partner will read one or two sentences from
the story. Listen and write.

_____

_____

_____

_____

3 Doing It in English: Talking about Work

A. What words describe Gloria Sierra's work? Check (✔) your opinion. Then tell the class.

Words to Describe Work

_____ easy _____ well paid

_____ hard/difficult _____ poorly paid

_____ interesting _____ relaxing

_____ not interesting/boring _____ stressful

_____ tiring

Add Other Words

dangerous

I think her job is easy!

I don't agree! I think...

B. What words describe the work in the photos on these pages? Tell the class your opinion.

© Ken Light

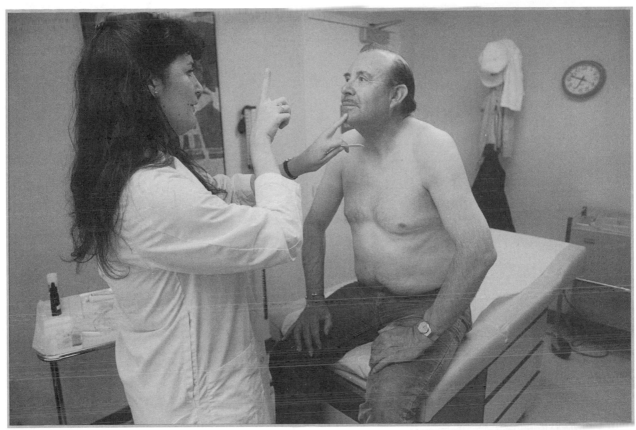

© Ken Light

C. Look back at Gloria's photo and story on page 52. What does she use to do her job? What do the workers on these pages use? What do you use? The Picture Dictionary below may help.

PICTURE DICTIONARY: Things We Use at Work		Add more words with the class.
Parts of the Body	**Tools**	
head	hammer	
eyes	drill	
hands	screwdriver	
arms	scissors	
legs	sewing machine	
back	computer	

4 Learning about Each Other: Our Work

Walk around your classroom. Talk to five people. Find out about their work and fill in the chart. (Remember that *student* and *homemaker* are also jobs!)

Sample Questions	Answers
What is your job?	I'm a bus driver.
What do you do?	I drive a school bus.
What hours do you work?	I work from 7 to 9 A.M. and 3 to 5 P.M.
Do you like your job?	Yes, I do. OR No, I don't.

Name	Job	Job Activities	Hours	Likes Job?
Gloria Sierra	bus driver	She drives a school bus and watches the children.	7-9 A.M. 3-5 P.M.	yes

What did you learn? Tell the class. Ask your classmates any questions you have about their work.

Why don't you like your job?

Gulshah is a clerk at Clothes Time. She sells clothes!

5 Listening in: Your Teacher's Work

Listen as your teacher tells you something about his or her job(s). Take notes below. Ask questions when you don't understand.

Teacher's name _____

Job(s) _____

Job activities _____

_____

Hours _____

Full-time or part-time? _____

One good thing about the job _____

One bad thing about the job _____

Tell a partner what you understood about your teacher.

Simple Present	
I You We They } **work** part-time.	He She } **works** part-time.
Use **simple present** for things you do every day or often.	

6 Bringing the Outside in: Interview Results

Interview a friend about his or her job. Ask the friend to tell you two good things and two bad things about the job. Discuss the answers with the class.

Friend's name _____

Friend's job _____

He/she likes _____

_____

He/she doesn't like _____

_____

Simple Present Negative	
I You We They } **don't** like it.	He She } **doesn't** like it.

7   More Stories from the Southwest

Read these two stories about work. Which person feels most like *you* do about work? Why? Tell the class.

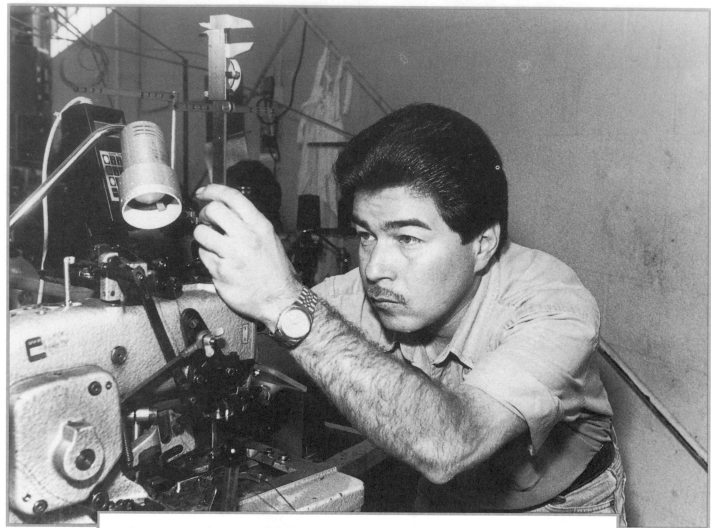

I am a sewing machine mechanic. I like this job because I use my head all the time. I like to help my coworkers. I was a sewing machine operator before, and I understand all their problems.

My job is sometimes stressful. There is a lot of pressure to do high-quality work. There is only one thing I don't like. It is when people get angry with me. Really, I always try to do my best for all the employees. My goal is to make everyone happy.

Jose Luis Garcia works at Levi Strauss in El Paso, TX. He studies ESL at El Paso Community College. He comes from Mexico.

IDIOMS
morning person
get mad

I start work at 5:00 in the morning. I'm a morning person. I have to be! I cook steak, eggs, bacon, and pancakes for breakfast. I have to watch the food carefully. Pancakes have to cook just two minutes on each side. Bacon has to cook five minutes on each side.

In the summer, I get dizzy from the heat in the kitchen. There aren't enough cooks here. That's the biggest problem. Sometimes I work ten hours, with no break. Sometimes I get mad. I want to quit. It's the same thing everyday. The same thing over and over. It's not an easy job.

Ramon Ramirez is from Mexico. He is a restaurant chef in New Mexico. He studies English at Santa Fe Community College.

Is your job stressful? Do you get mad at work? Tell the class.

 Circle new words in the stories. Talk to a partner about the words. Read one story aloud to a partner.

8 Journal Writing

Ramon Ramirez sometimes gets mad at work.
Do you ever get mad when you work
(at your job, at home, or at school)?
What makes you mad? What do you do
when you are mad?

Answer these questions in your journal.
Ask your teacher a question.

This is what one student wrote.

I work in an office. I get
a lot of telephone calls
in Spanish and English.
I get mad when people
are impolite or rude on
the phone. Why can't
people say "please" and
"thank you"?

9 Ideas for Action: Solving Problems at Work

There aren't enough cooks here. That's
the biggest problem. Sometimes I work
ten hours with no break. Sometimes I get
mad. I want to quit.

 **A.** Ramon has some problems at work.
With a group, write some suggestions.

1. _He should ask the boss for a break._

2. _____

3. _____

B. What other problems do people have at work?
Write some ideas with your group.

1. _____

2. _____

3. _____

Talk about solutions with the class.

10 Doing It in English: Thinking of Jobs That Suit Us

A. Fill out the chart below with information about five friends or family members. The Picture Dictionary below may help.

Name of Friend or Family Member	Job	Likes It?

 Tell a partner about these people.

> My brother is an electrician. He likes his job.

NOTE: a or an?

a musician	an architect
a farmer	an actor
a cook	an engineer

PICTURE DICTIONARY: Jobs | **Add more words with the class.**

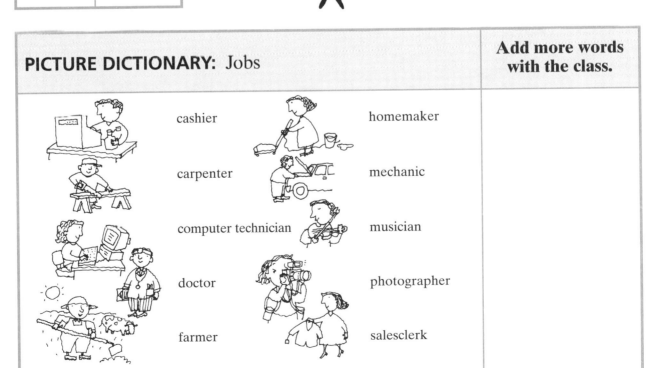

cashier

carpenter

computer technician

doctor

farmer

homemaker

mechanic

musician

photographer

salesclerk

B. Look at all the jobs listed in Exercise A. Put these jobs (and any others) into the three categories below.

Very Interesting to Me	Interesting to Me	Not Interesting to Me

 Discuss your lists with a partner. Are they similar? Ask each other any questions you have.

11 Then and Now: Comparing Jobs

 Tell a partner about your past, present, and future jobs. Fill in the chart.

	Past	Now	Future
	I was …	*I am …*	*I would like to be …*
I			
My Partner			

Be	
present	**past**
I **am**	I **was**
you **are**	you **were**
he, she, it **is**	he, she, it **was**
we **are**	we **were**
they **are**	they **were**

What steps can you take to get this job?

I don't talk much English. My boss speaks to me in Spanish. With customers I speak the little English I know. I don't have any problems.

Arturo Castillo (left) is from Mexico. He is a furniture maker in Albuquerque, NM. He is with his boss, George Sandoval.

A. Arturo doesn't need much English at work. What about you? How much English do you need at work? For what? Tell the class.

B. Think about jobs in your community. How much English do they require? Make lists with the class or a group.

Jobs That Require No English	Jobs That Require Some English	Jobs That Require a Lot of English

C. Circle a job you would like to have in the future.

13 Other Voices from North America

Choose one or two stories to read. Is the writer like you or someone you know? Tell a partner.

In Portugal, my father made medicine out of seaweed and sold it to the hospitals. Here he makes his own wine. He works in the cemetery during the week and fishes on weekends. He worked hard to bring all of us here.

Al Laurencio (far right) lives in Massachusetts with his family.

WORDS I WANT TO REMEMBER

IDIOM
spend time

I am from India. I work in my house. In India, housework is difficult. Here it is easier. I get up at 6 a.m. and make breakfast and lunch. Then I come to school. After school, I go home and clean the bathroom, the windows, and other things. Then I go to the store and buy groceries. I sew clothes. I make chapatties and other Indian food. I have many responsibilities on my head. My husband only has to work at one thing—his job.

Gill Sukhwinder studies ESL at Invergarry Language Centre, Vancouver, British Columbia, Canada.

I sew at a factory in Chinatown. Every day I need to work more than ten hours. Sometimes I work seven days a week. I feel very tired after work. I don't like this job because I get little money but spend a lot of time.

I want to find an office job, but now I have too many problems in English. I don't have the courage to interview for another job.

Huan Ying Li is from China. She studies ESL at LaGuardia Community College in New York City.

14 Options for Learning: English at Work

> I want to talk to the American people at work. That's why I'm studying English.

Robert Salas, El Paso Community College

A. How do you want to use English at work?
Check (✔) your answer. Add other ideas if you wish.

	Already Do	Want to Learn	Not Interested
To understand warnings at work	_____	_____	_____
To call in sick to work	_____	_____	_____
To report problems to my boss	_____	_____	_____
To read job ads in the newspaper	_____	_____	_____
(Other) _____	_____	_____	_____
_____	_____	_____	_____

 B. Talk to a partner or group about your learning goals. Use your native language if you wish. Tell the class in English.

C. Ask your teacher for a *Collaborations* worksheet on one of these goals.

15 Looking Back

Think about your learning. Fill in the blanks. Then tell the class your ideas.

A. In this unit I learned _____

_____.

B. I want to study more about _____.

C. The activity I liked best was 1 2 3 4 5 6 7 8 9 10 11 12 13 14

because _____.

D. The activity I liked least was 1 2 3 4 5 6 7 8 9 10 11 12 13 14

because _____.

Checklist for Learning

I. Vocabulary: Check (✔) the words you know. Add more words if you wish.

I can Describe Work	Jobs	Things We Use at Work:	
		Body Parts	**Tools**
_____ easy	_____ bus driver	_____ head	_____ hammer
_____ hard	_____ chef	_____ eyes	_____ drill
_____ difficult	_____ mechanic	_____ hands	_____ screwdriver
_____ interesting	_____ computer	_____ arms	_____ scissors
_____ boring	_____ technician	_____ legs	_____ sewing machine
_____ well paid	_____ carpenter	_____ back	_____ computer
_____ poorly paid	_____ photographer	_____ _____	_____ _____
_____ relaxing	_____ cashier	_____ _____	_____ _____
_____ stressful	_____ homemaker	_____ _____	_____ _____
_____ tiring	_____ doctor		
_____ dangerous	_____ farmer		
_____ _____	_____ musician	**IDOMS**	
_____ _____	_____ teacher	_____ knock on wood	
_____ _____	_____ salesclerk	_____ morning person	
_____ _____	_____ electrician	_____ get mad	
		_____ spend time	

II. Language: Check (✔) what you can do in English. Add more ideas if you wish.

I can

_____ describe my job.

_____ tell what I do at work.

_____ tell what I use at work.

_____ read short stories.

_____ name the parts of the body.

_____ tell what jobs are interesting or boring to me.

_____ tell what makes me mad at work.

_____ tell some solutions to problems at work.

_____ _____

III. Listening: Listen to the Review Interview at the end of Unit 4. Ask your teacher for a *Collaborations* worksheet.

Getting and Giving Help: Stories from Virginia

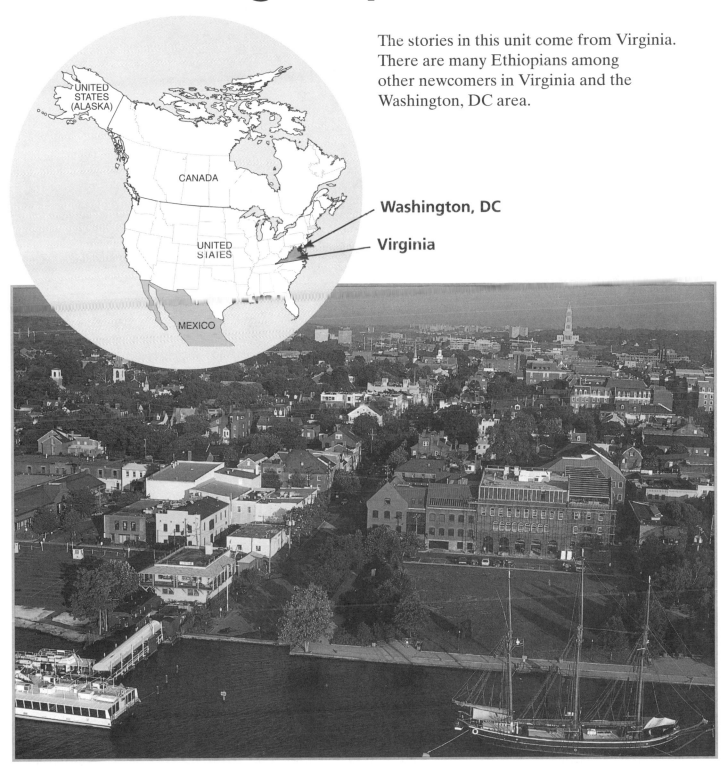

The stories in this unit come from Virginia. There are many Ethiopians among other newcomers in Virginia and the Washington, DC area.

Washington, DC

Virginia

Tekola Beyene's Story

In Alexandria, the houses are not close to each other. Everyone has their own yard. You don't even know the names of your neighbors. Some people say hello on the street. But others don't talk. They are afraid because I am a Black person. There are some old women on my block. They rake their own leaves! Nobody helps them.

In Ethiopia, everybody knew each other. My sons played in neighbors' houses every day. If we lived on the same block, we talked, visited, and drank coffee together. We never let an old person do work! If you needed help, someone was always there!

Tekola Beyene is from Ethiopia. Now he lives in Alexandria, VA, with his wife and sons.

- Do you help your neighbors?

- Do they help you?

2 Playing with Story Language

A. Listen to the story.

B. Listen again and write the missing words.

In Alexandria, the houses _____ not close to each other. Everyone
                              1

_____ their own yard. You don't even _____ the names of your
      2   3

neighbors. Some people _____ hello on the street. But others don't
                              4

_____. Some people are afraid because I _____ a Black person.
      5   6

There _____ some old women on my block. They _____ their own
          7   8

leaves! Nobody _____ them.
                      9

In Ethiopia, everybody _____ each other. My sons _____ in
                              10   11

neighbors' houses every day. If we _____ on the same block, we talked,
                                          12

_____, and drank coffee together. We never _____ an old person
      13   14

do work! If you _____ help, someone _____ always there!
                      15   16

Show your answers to a classmate. Do you agree? Check your answers.

C. Challenge: Cover the story. Your teacher or classmate will read one
or two sentences. Listen and write. Then check your writing.

_____

_____

_____

_____

3 Doing It in English: Talking about Neighbors

Simple Present Questions	
Do I / you / we / they } **live** in a house?	**Does** he / she } **live** in a house?

A. Check (✔) your answer in column 1.

		1 Me YES NO	2 My Partner YES NO
Do you	live in an apartment building?	❑ ❑	❑ ❑
	live in a house?	❑ ❑	❑ ❑
	say hi to your neighbors?	❑ ❑	❑ ❑
	like your neighbors?	❑ ❑	❑ ❑
	know your neighbors well?	❑ ❑	❑ ❑
	visit your neighbors?	❑ ❑	❑ ❑
	help your neighbors?	❑ ❑	❑ ❑
Do your neighbors	speak your language?	❑ ❑	❑ ❑
	speak English?	❑ ❑	❑ ❑
	help you?	❑ ❑	❑ ❑
	ask you for help?	❑ ❑	❑ ❑

B. Ask your partner these questions. Check (✔) his or her answer in column 2.

Do you live in an apartment building?

Yes, I do.

Do you live in a house?

No, I don't.

C. Ask more about your partner's neighbors.

Where are your neighbors from?

El Salvador.

4 Listening in: Your Teacher's Neighbors

A. Your teacher will talk about his or her neighbors. Listen carefully!
Check **YES** or **NO** as you listen.

		YES	NO
Does your teacher	live in an apartment building?	❏	❏
	live in a house?	❏	❏
	say hi to his/her neighbors?	❏	❏
	like his/her neighbors?	❏	❏
	know his/her neighbors well?	❏	❏
	visit his/her neighbors?	❏	❏
	help his/her neighbors?	❏	❏
Do your teacher's neighbors	speak English?	❏	❏
	speak another language	❏	❏
	help your teacher?	❏	❏
	ask your teacher for help?	❏	❏

Other Notes

_____

_____

What did you learn about your teacher's neighbors? Tell a partner.

B. Do you want to know more? With your partner, write two questions.
Ask your teacher!

Example: ___Where are your neighbors from?_____

1. _____

2. _____

A. Think about neighbors here and in your native country.

Write **YES** or **NO** in each column.

	Here	In My Native Country
Are neighbors friendly?		
Do they say *hello* or *good morning?*		
Do they visit each other?		
Do they drink coffee together?		
Do neighbors help each other?		
Do they rake leaves or help in the yard?		
Do they watch each other's children?		
Do they give each other food?		
Do they watch the house or apartment when someone is away?		

 Share your answers with a partner or the class.

B. How else are neighbors the same or different in North America and your country? Write your answer.

In my native country, neighbors _____.

In this country, neighbors _____.

 Tell a partner or the class.

6 Journal Writing

Write to your teacher about your neighbors here or in your native country. Ask your teacher about his or her neighbors.

Here is what a student in Fairfax, VA, wrote.

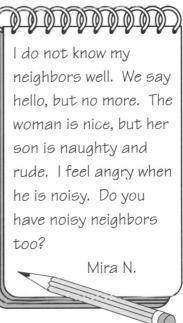

I do not know my neighbors well. We say hello, but no more. The woman is nice, but her son is naughty and rude. I feel angry when he is noisy. Do you have noisy neighbors too?

Mira N.

7 Ideas for Action: Getting to Know Your Neighbors

How can you get to know your neighbors? With your class, write some ideas. What can you offer or ask for? What can you invite them to do?

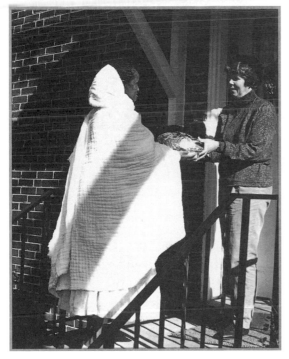

1. We can offer food from our country.

2. _____

3. _____

4. _____

What can you say to your neighbors?
Roleplay with the class.

Would you like to taste a samosa?

What is it?

It's like a meat pastry.

Thanks!

Would you like to come for tea this afternoon?

Yes. I'd like to. What time?

About 3 o'clock?

Thanks. See you then.

More Stories from Virginia

Read Tekola's stories about arriving in Virginia. Are you like anyone in these stories?

When I arrived in America, there weren't many Ethiopians here. There were no organizations like the Ethiopian Community Center. There were no Ethiopian restaurants or stores. I didn't know anyone from my country.

Russ and Polly lived in Ethiopia a long time ago. They were in the Peace Corps. When they heard I was coming to America, they invited me to live in their house. They helped me with everything. Now my wife and sons live here too. Some day, I will repay their kindness.

Russ and Polly Scoville live in Alexandria, VA. In this photo, Tekola is talking with them in their kitchen.

When you first arrived, who helped you? How?

Do you help newcomers? How? Tell the class.

Now, there are many Ethiopians here. Newcomers can often find friends or relatives at Ethiopian stores and restaurants. There are organizations like the Red Cross and the Ethiopian Community Center that can help with housing.

One older man I know couldn't get along with his brother. He called me. I helped him find a house. I gave him a little money, too. We must help our countrymen! He's all settled now.

This family has just arrived from Ethiopia.
Tekola (far right) is helping them, too.

IDIOMS
get along with
be all settled

 Circle new words in the stories. Talk to a partner about the words. Which story do you like? Tell why.

Doing It in English: Getting Help in the Community

A. Which of these community services have you used? Add other services if you can.

PICTURE DICTIONARY: Services	Add more words with the class.
police station Red Cross fire station bus ambulance train poison helpline ethnic center	

B. With your class, fill in the chart below. Use phone books to find the phone numbers. Add other community services at the bottom of the chart.

	Phone Number	Help Offered
Help:		
general emergency	911	help with all emergencies
fire station		
ambulance		
police department		
Information:		
bus		
train		
subway		
Other Important Places:		

Please help me! There's someone in my house!

What's your name?

Ana Alvarez

What's your address?

4524 Belleview. Please hurry!

C. Which services speak your language? Put a check next to the service.

D. Do you know how to make a phone call in English? Practice with a partner as in the example.

Bringing the Outside in: Community Resources

With your class, choose a service from your chart on page 76.
Tell your classmates what you know about it.
What do you want to know? Make a list of questions.

Invite someone from that service to
come and speak to your class.

Practice your questions before
the guest speaker arrives.
If you don't understand the speaker,
ask questions!

Would you repeat that please?

Students at Project REEP learned
about the police at the Arlington
County Fair in Virginia.

Thinking about Language Use: In Your Community

This map shows my neighborhood. Mostly white people live here. There is one Ethiopian family three blocks away. Most Ethiopians live in Washington, DC. I have to drive for ninety minutes to get there. I like to go, because there are stores and restaurants where they speak Ahmaric. I can hear familiar sounds and see familiar faces.

Tekola Beyene

Draw a map of your neighborhood. Put a star (*) on your home. Write an "X" where people from your country live. Where can you go to hear familiar sounds and see familiar faces?

12 Other Voices from North America

Choose one story to read.
Is the writer like you or someone you know?
Tell a partner.

My next door neighbors are African-American people. They have two children. They are friendly. Every time we meet I say *hi*. They say *hi* back to me and they always smile. Sometimes they lend eggs to us. Sometimes they borrow milk from us.

They are nice people but we haven't talked much because my English isn't very good.

Pijen Liang studies English in Northhampton, MA.
She is from Taiwan.

WORDS I WANT TO REMEMBER

I help my friends and neighbors when they arrive in Miami from Cuba. They don't know English, and I do. I help them fill in immigration forms, and I help them enroll in school.

There are so many barriers here. You have to do so many things you have never done before. We all need to help each other.

Avelino Gonzalez studies English at the University of Miami, FL. He is from Cuba.

13

Learning about Each Other: Discovering Resources

My teeth hurt every day. I can't eat or sleep well. It is hard to study English. I can't finish my homework.

I went to the dentist. He is my friend. He likes watercolor paintings very much. He said, "You don't have to pay money." He agreed to fix my teeth. He pulled out my bad teeth. After that I felt better! The dentist told me to brush my teeth and not to smoke my pipe too much. I gave him a watercolor painting, instead of paying $200.

Dirk Xu studies English in Massachusetts.
He is from China.

Dirk and his dentist made a trade. Do you make trades?

Lynda Terrill's class at Project REEP in Arlington, VA, made the list below.

Think about trading help with your classmates. What help do you need? What help will you give?

Put checks (✔) in the correct columns.

		I Want Help with This	I Will Offer Help with This
1.	English	✔	
2.	My language		✔
3.	Sewing		
4.	Using computers		
5.	Babysitting		
6.	Cooking		
7.	How to swim		
8.	How to play soccer		
9.	(other)		
10.	(other)		

 Talk with a partner.
What two services do you want?
What two services will you offer?

Joining Two Sentences with *or*
I will baby sit **or** I will cook.
I will fix cars **or** I will plant flowers.

Collaborations: Making a Trading Post

With your class, make a bulletin board with two sides. Write your name, address, and telephone number on a card. Write what you will do for someone or what you need. Pin your card on the *Help Offered* side or on the *Help Wanted* side.

Your Name, Address, and Phone Number		Your Name, Address, and Phone Number
I will . . .	OR	I need . . .

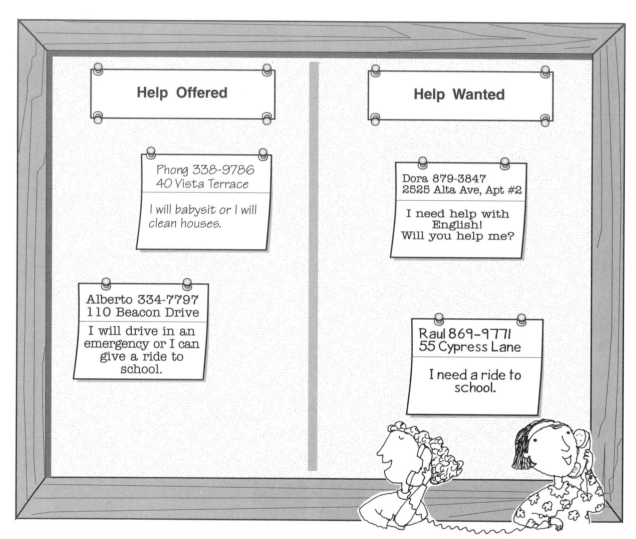

Help Offered

Phong 338-9786
40 Vista Terrace

I will babysit or I will clean houses.

Alberto 334-7797
110 Beacon Drive

I will drive in an emergency or I can give a ride to school.

Help Wanted

Dora 879-3847
2525 Alta Ave, Apt #2

I need help with English!
Will you help me?

Raul 869-9771
55 Cypress Lane

I need a ride to school.

Future: Long and Short Forms		
I **will**		I**'ll**
You **will**		You**'ll**
She/he **will**	cook.	She**'ll**/he**'ll**	cook.
We **will**		We**'ll**
They **will**		They**'ll**

When you finish, call your classmates!

15 Options for Learning: English in Your Neighborhood

A. How do you want to use English in your neighborhood? Check (✔) your answers. Add other ideas if you wish.

	Already Do	Want to Learn	Not Interested
To talk to neighbors	_____	_____	_____
To read signs in my neighborhood	_____	_____	_____
To call the police or fire department	_____	_____	_____
To read transportation schedules	_____	_____	_____
Other _____	_____	_____	_____
	_____	_____	_____

 B. Talk to your classmates or your group about your learning goals Use your language if you wish. Tell the class in English.

C. Ask your teacher for a *Collaborations* worksheet on one of these goals.

16 Looking Back

Think about your learning. Fill in the blanks. Then tell the class your ideas.

A. In this unit I learned _____

_____ .

B. I want to study more about _____ .

C. The activity I liked best was 1 2 3 4 5 6 7 8 9 10 11 12 13 14 15

because _____ .

D. The activity I liked least was 1 2 3 4 5 6 7 8 9 10 11 12 13 14 15

because _____ .

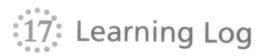

Checklist for Learning

I. Vocabulary: Check (✔) the words you know. Add more words if you wish.

Neighborhood Words and Phrases

Nouns

_____ house
_____ apartment
_____ yard
_____ neighbor
_____ block

_____ _____

_____ _____

Services and Transportation

_____ 911 (emergency)
_____ police
_____ fire department
_____ ambulance
_____ bus, train, subway
_____ Red Cross

_____ _____

_____ _____

_____ _____

Verbs and Verbs Phrases

_____ help
_____ visit
_____ play
_____ rake leaves
_____ drink coffee
_____ say hello
_____ watch children
_____ offer food

_____ _____

_____ _____

_____ _____

IDIOMS

_____ get along with
_____ be all settled

II. Language: Check (✔) what you can do in English. Add more ideas if you wish.

I can

_____ ask questions about neighbors
and neighborhoods.
_____ tell about my neighbors.
_____ read short stories.
_____ understand my teacher's stories.
_____ call 911.

_____ call the police.
_____ call the fire department.
_____ offer and ask for help from a
neighbor.
_____ offer and ask for help from
classmates.

III. Listening: Listen to the Review Interview at the end of Unit 5. Ask your
teacher for a *Collaborations* worksheet.

Unit 6

New Culture, New Ways: Stories from Vancouver

The stories in this unit come from Vancouver, British Columbia, Canada. Tens of thousands of immigrants and refugees from all over the world have settled in Vancouver.

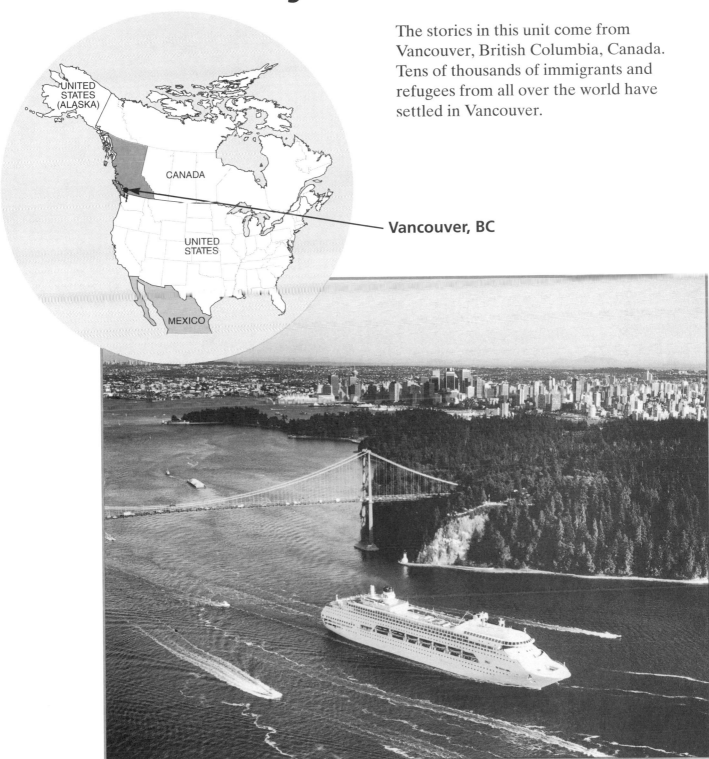

Vancouver, BC

Sun Park's Story

When I came to Canada, I saw some men and women kiss each other in the restaurant, on the street, and in the school yard. I was shocked! In this country, men and women live together outside of marriage. This would never happen in Korea! I told my children, "Please don't learn this custom." There are so many broken homes here. In Korea, families are stronger. I worry about my children's and my grandchildren's future.

Sun Park studies in the Bridge Program in Vancouver, British Columbia, Canada. She is from Korea.

• When you first arrived, what surprised you?

IDIOM
broken homes

2 Playing with Story Language

A. Listen to the story.

B. Work with a partner. Cover the story. One person reads, and the other writes the missing words.

When I _____ to Canada, I saw some women and men _____ each other in the
            1   2

restaurant, on the street, and in the school yard. I _____ shocked! In this country, men
                                                          3

and women _____ together outside of marriage. This would never _____ in
                    4   5

Korea. I _____ my children, "Please don't _____ this custom." There
              6   7

_____ so many broken homes here. In Korea, families _____ stronger.
        8   9

C. Change roles. One person reads, and the other writes the missing words.

When _____ came to Canada, I saw some _____ and men kiss each other in
            1   2

the restaurant, on the _____, and in the school yard. I was shocked! In this country,
                              3

_____ and women live together outside of _____. This would never happen
        4   5

in _____! I told my children, "Please don't learn this _____." There are so
        6   7

many broken _____ here. In Korea, _____ are stronger.
                    8   9

Show your answers to a classmate. Do you agree? Check your answers.

D. Challenge: Cover the story. Your teacher or partner will read the
last sentence on p. 84. Listen and write. Then check your writing.

_____

_____

3 Doing It in English: Talking about First Impressions

A. Think about your first days
in your new country. What did
you see? How did you feel?

Write your answers.
The Picture Dictionary below may help.

People here feed pets in the house. I was really surprised.

Susan Lai is from Taiwan.

What Did You See?	How Did You Feel?

PICTURE DICTIONARY: Feelings | **Add more words with the class.**

surprised

shocked

upset

puzzled

happy

amused

worried

embarrassed

B. Ask your partner about his
or her first days in this
country. Use words
and phrases from the
box to show you are listening.

What did you see?

I saw a homeless man in the street.

Oh! How did you feel?

I was really shocked.

I know what you mean.

Listening Phrases

Oh.
Really?
Wow!
I see.
I know what you
    mean.
Tell me more.

Tell the class about your partner.

4 **Listening in:** Your Teacher's First Impressions

A. Your teacher will talk about his or her first impressions of a new country or a new place. Listen carefully. Take notes on your teacher's story.

My Teacher's Trip

Where did he/she go? _____

When did he/she go? _____

What did he/she see?   How did he/she feel?

1. _____   _____

2. _____   _____

3. _____   _____

Other information

_____

_____

 What did you learn about your teacher? Tell a partner.

B. Do you want to know more? With your partner, write three questions. Ask your teacher!

1. _____

2. _____

3. _____

 Why did you go to China?

Simple Past Questions	
Where **did** you **go**?	I **went** to China.
When **did** you **go**?	I **went** in May.
What **did** you **see**?	I **saw** a lot of bicycles!

5 More Stories from Vancouver

Learners at Invergarry Learning Centre in Vancouver were surprised about many things when they first arrived in Canada. Look at the photos. Read the stories. Which things surprised you, too? Put a check (✔) next to them.

I heard my sister say "I'm sorry" to her son. I was shocked. In my country, young people are very polite to old people. Even if parents or old people make mistakes, they don't say "sorry" to children.

Thanh Giang, South Vietnam

One day I was at the bus stop. I saw two women kissing on the mouth. I felt surprised and confused. I didn't believe what I saw! One women saw me and winked her eye and laughed at me. They were crazy.

Gerrara Tonalisa, Peru

In Canada, so many things surprised me. People feed pets in the house! Children here play a lot. They are very happy. But old people are very lonely.

Susan Lai, Taiwan

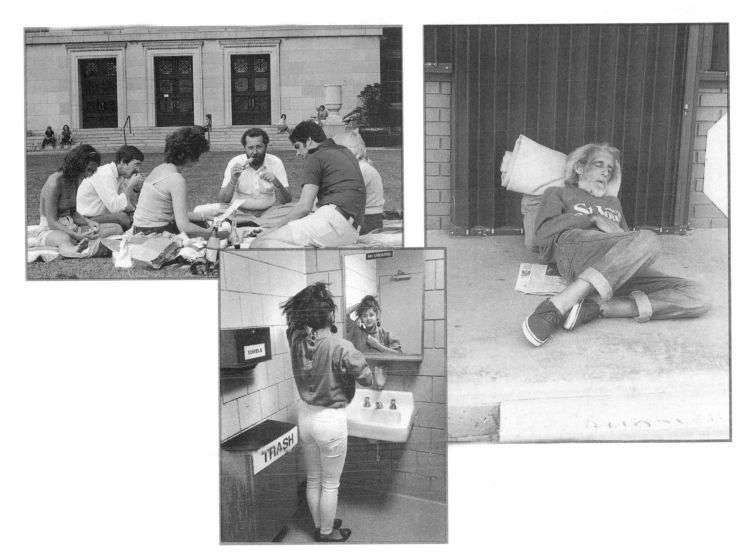

In my country, eating is a polite custom. Canadians eat anywhere at lunch break. I see Canadians sitting, standing, or even lying down in the park to enjoy their meals.

Susie Kim, South Korea

In my country, parents have authority over children. Here, the government protects children too much. If you punish your children, someone can call the police or the social worker! This shocked me. The parents are afraid to punish their children.

Gladys Escalante, El Salvador

I was shocked to hear that Canadians don't leave children under age 12 home alone. If you leave children alone, neighbors call the police!

Amy Hsu, Taiwan

In Canada, children watch too much TV, they don't study much, they spend too much money, and they like to smoke cigarettes! In my country, children respect their parents. They don't leave when they are 18—they stay in their houses with their parents for their whole lives.

Dhangauri Ganderia, India

Other Voices from North America

These stories are told by students of San Francisco State University, in San Francisco, CA. Choose one or two stories to read. Is the story like your story?

When I came to San Francisco, I was very surprised by how people talk. For example, on the street or in the bus, strangers say *hi* when you don't even know them! In my country, you only greet people you know.

Sang Kil, South Korea

I was surprised that Americans like to sunbathe. They think the tan color of skin is beautiful. In my country, women want their skin as white as possible. We use umbrellas to keep the sun off our faces.

Vivian Wong, Hong Kong

When I arrived in my new neighborhood, I saw flowers beside every house. I was surprised! By the roadside, the flowers look beautiful. It made me feel happy to see pretty flowers every day.

Yi-Lieu Hsu, Taiwan

I was so surprised when I saw homeless people. They have shopping carts with plastic bags and cans. They always ask me for money. We try to ignore these people, but this could happen to any of us.

Raoul de Vaucelles, France

WORDS I WANT TO REMEMBER

Doing It in English: Talking about Reactions

The students in Vancouver and San Francisco were surprised by these things. What about you? Check (✔) your answer.

	I was. . . .	not surprised	surprised	shocked
Greetings	Some people say hi to strangers.			
Eating	Some people eat in the park, sitting or standing.			
Clothing and Beauty	Some people wear bikini swimsuits in public.			
	Some people like to sunbathe. They like to have tanned skin.			
Streets and Surroundings	In some places, there are flowers on the street.			
	There are some homeless people on the street.			
Animals & Pets	Some people let pets eat in the kitchen.			
Families	Old people seem lonely.			
	Some old people are friendly to young people.			
	Parents say "I'm sorry" to children.			
Rules and Laws	Parents must not leave children home alone.			
	Parents must not hit their children.			

 Show your answers to a partner.
Which answers are different? Find out why.

Must/Must Not
must = It is necessary. must not = Do not do this!
You **must** have someone watch your children. You **must not** leave your children home alone.

Why were you shocked about bikinis?

Because in my country, women must cover their bodies.

8 Learning about Each Other: Things That Surprise Us

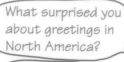

What surprised you about greetings in North America?

Strangers say hello to you!

What surprised your classmates about North America?
Work with a small group. Ask each other questions.
Find one example from someone in your group for each category.

Category	Name	Native Country	What Surprised This Person?
Greetings	Sang	Korea	Strangers say hello
Greetings			
Eating			
Clothing and Beauty			
Streets and Surroundings			
Animals and Pets			
Families			
Rules and Laws			

9 Bringing the Outside in: Pictures for a Wall Display

With your class, make your own collage like the one on pages 88–89.

Bring pictures of things that surprise you about the United States or Canada. Look in magazines. Do you have a camera? Take some photos!

Copy quotes from the chart above onto index cards. Make a wall display. Put pictures and photos on the top and quotes on the bottom.

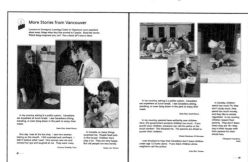

Then and Now: Comparing Customs

A. Think about customs in your native country and customs in this
country. What is the same? Write your answers.

In this country, people eat outside in the park,
and in my native country, we eat outside **too.**

In this country, women don't wear veils,
and in my native country, women don't wear
them **either.**

Combining Sentences
(positive sentence), **and** (positive sentence) **too.**
(negative sentence), **and** (negative sentence) **either.**

Same

In this country, people _____

    and in my native country, _____ **too.**

In this country, people don't _____

    and in my native country, _____ **either.**

B. What is different? Write your answers.

Different

In this country, people _____

    but in my native country, _____ .

In this country, people don't _____

    but in my native country, _____ .

Journal Writing

Choose one sentence from part B. Copy it in your
journal. Write more about it for your teacher. Ask
your teacher a question if you wish.

In this country, all
people drive cars
(even old people),
but in my native
country, few people
drive. Why don't
people walk much?

          Mei Ling

12 Doing It in English: Teaching about Customs in Your Country

How do people greet each other? Brainstorm with the class. The Picture Dictionary may help.

PICTURE DICTIONARY: Ways of Greeting (Verbs)		**Add more words with the class.**
smile hug		
wave kiss on cheek		
bow kiss on both cheeks		
shake hands		

 A. Work with classmates from your country. Show the class how people in your country greet these people.

> a family member
> an old friend
> a new acquaintance
> a boss
> a co-worker
> a foreigner

How is this the same in North America? How is it different? Tell your classmates.

 B. North Americans often give compliments on clothes, appearance, and other things.

I like your dress.

Thanks!

Is this similar or different from your native country? Talk with your group. Use your native language if you wish. Then tell the class in English.

 C. Tell your group about a custom in your country that would surprise them.

Options for Learning: North American Customs

> In my country, a young girl of 15 does not go out alone at night. Her mother or brother or older sister goes with her. But teenagers here do anything! I wonder why parents let them?

Julie Garcia studies at Invergarry Learning Centre in Vancouver. She's from Guatemala.

A. What do you want to know more about? Check (✔) your answer.

North American Custom	Want to Learn About	Already Know	Not Interested
Greetings	_____	_____	_____
Giving compliments	_____	_____	_____
Dating and courtship	_____	_____	_____
Attitudes towards pets	_____	_____	_____
(Other) _____	_____	_____	_____
_____	_____	_____	_____

B. Talk with a small group. Use your language if you wish. What do you want to learn more about?

C. Ask your teacher for a *Collaborations* worksheet on one of these areas.

D. Invite a guest speaker to your class. Ask about his/her travels to other countries. Ask about North American customs you don't understand.

Collaborations: Making a Handbook for Newcomers

 With a small group, make a handbook, or "survival guide" for new students. Each group will write about one category from the chart on p. 91.

Learn as much as you can. Ask your teacher, other North Americans, and people from your country who have been here for a long time, this question: *When people come from other countries, what should they know about North Americans?*

Write a page for the handbook.

Category _____

Authors _____

    In this country, North Americans [tell how they do it]_____

_____

_____

    This surprised us because we [give examples from your countries] _____

_____

_____

    In general, we suggest that you _____

_____

_____

With your classmates, look again at your page. What else should go in? What should come out? What corrections do you want to make? Decide together and revise what you wrote.

Rewrite your page with the changes. Make the book with your class.

Who should read it? Share what you learned with new students.

15 Ideas for Action: Learning about Different Cultures

> Koreans and Canadians have different cultures. But I don't think either one is good or bad—it is just different. Koreans have to respect Canadian culture. Canadians have to respect Korean culture. Differences can be very beautiful. When we understand each other we can make good lives together.
>
> Mary Koh studies at the School Bridge Program in Vancouver. She is from South Korea.

How can you learn more about customs of your new community?

How can you teach people more about the customs of your native country?

With your class, write two ideas.

Ways to Learn:

1. _____Make American friends._____

2. _____

3. _____

Ways to Teach:

1. _Invite Americans to native holidays._

2. _____

3. _____

16 Looking Back

Think about your learning. Fill in the blanks.
Then tell the class your ideas.

> **A.** In this unit I learned _____
>
> _____.
>
> **B.** I want to study more about _____.
>
> **C.** The activity I liked best was 1 2 3 4 5 6 7 8 9 10 11 12 13 14 15
>
> because _____.
>
> **D.** The activity I liked least was 1 2 3 4 5 6 7 8 9 10 11 12 13 14 15
>
> because _____.

Checklist for Learning

I. Vocabulary: Check (✔) the words you know. Add more words if you wish.

Feelings

_____ surprised
_____ upset
_____ happy
_____ worried
_____ shocked
_____ puzzled
_____ amused
_____ embarrassed

_____ _____
_____ _____

Ways of Greeting

_____ wave
_____ shake hands
_____ bow
_____ kiss
_____ hug
_____ smile

_____ _____
_____ _____

IDIOMS
_____ broken homes
_____ take a sunbath

II. Language: Check (✔) what you can do in English. Add more ideas if you wish.

I can

_____ greet people in English.
_____ give a compliment.
_____ read short stories.
_____ understand my teacher's stories.
_____ use listening phrases to keep a conversation going.
_____ talk about what surprised me when I arrived in North America.
_____ talk about customs in North America.
_____ talk about customs in my native country.

_____ _____
_____ _____

III. Listening: Listen to the Review Interview at the end of Unit 6. Ask your
teacher for the *Collaborations* worksheet.

INDEX

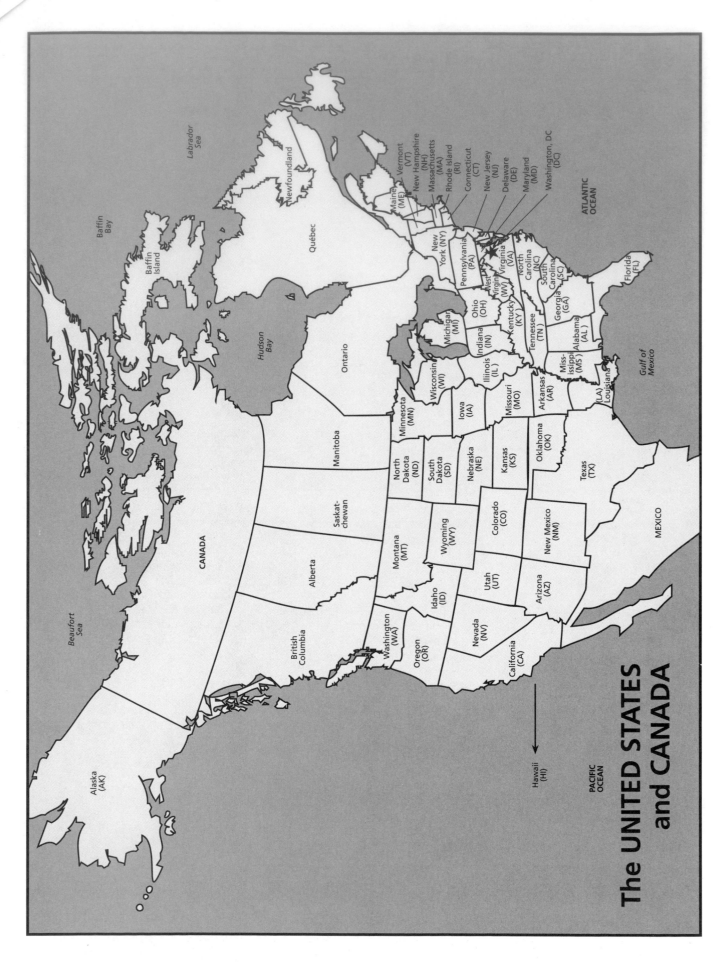

The UNITED STATES and CANADA